The
Reasons
of Love

Harry G. Frankfurt

Princeton University Press

Princeton and Oxford

Copyright © 2004 by Princeton University Press
Published by Princeton University Press,
41 William Street, Princeton, New Jersey 08540
In the United Kingdom: Princeton University Press,
3 Market Place, Woodstock, Oxfordshire OX20 1SY

Fourth printing, and first paperback printing, 2006
Paperback ISBN-13: 978-0-691-12624-1
Paperback ISBN-10: 0-691-12624-0

The Library of Congress has cataloged the cloth edition of this book as follows

Frankfurt, Harry G., 1929–
The reasons of love / Harry G. Frankfurt.
p.   cm.
Includes bibliographical references.
ISBN 0-691-09164-1 (alk. paper)
1. Practical reason. 2. Love. I. Title.
BC177.F69   2004
177′.7—dc21   2003050428

British Library Cataloging-in-Publication Data is available

This book has been composed in Adobe Caslon

Printed on acid-free paper. ∞

pup.princeton.edu

Printed in the United States of America

9   10

The Reasons of Love

Contents

Contents

The Reasons of Love

One

The Question: "How Should We Live?"

1 We have it on the authority both of Plato and of Aristotle that philosophy began in wonder. People wondered about various natural phenomena that they found surprising. They also puzzled over what struck them as curiously recalcitrant logical, or linguistic, or conceptual problems that turned up unexpectedly in the course of their thinking. As an example of what led him to wonder, Socrates mentions the fact that it is possible for one person to become shorter than another without shrinking in height. We might wonder why Socrates should have been made at all uncomfortable by such a shallow paradox. Evidently the problem struck him not only as more interesting, but also as considerably more difficult and disturbing, than it strikes us. Indeed, referring to this problem and others like it, he says, "Sometimes I get quite dizzy with thinking of them."[1]

Aristotle gives a list of several rather more compelling examples of the sorts of things by which the first philosophers were led to wonder. He mentions self-moving marionettes (apparently the Greeks had them!); he mentions certain cosmological and astronomical phenomena; and he mentions the fact that the side of a square is incommensurable with the diagonal. It is hardly appropriate to characterize these things merely as puzzling. They are startling. They are marvels. The response they inspired must have been deeper, and more unsettling, than simply—as Aristotle puts it—a "wondering that the matter is so."[2] It must have been resonant with feelings of mystery, of the uncanny, of awe.

Whether the earliest philosophers were trying to fathom the secrets of the universe, or just trying to figure out how

---

[1] *Theaetetus* 155d.

[2] All of my quotations in this chapter from Aristotle are from his *Metaphysics* 982–83.

to think clearly about some quite ordinary fact or how to express some commonplace observation accurately, Aristotle reports that their inquiries had no further and more practical goals. They were eager to overcome their ignorance, but that was not because they thought they needed the information. In fact, their ambition was exclusively speculative or theoretical. They wanted nothing more than to dispel their initial surprise that things are as they are, by developing a reasoned understanding of why it would be unnatural—or even impossible—for things to be any other way. When it becomes clear that something was only to be expected, that dissipates whatever sense of surprise it may initially have engendered. As Aristotle remarks concerning right triangles, "there is nothing which would surprise a *geometer* so much as if the diagonal turned out to *be* commensurable."[3]

I am going to be concerned here with, among other things, certain discomforts and disturbances by which human beings are rather typically beset. These differ both from the sorts of discomforts and disturbances that may be caused by logical difficulties, such as the one Socrates mentions, and from those that tend to arise in response to fea-

---

[3] Aristotle is talking here, of course, about the Pythagorean theorem. There is a nice story about this. When Pythagoras made his extraordinary discovery, he was profoundly shaken by the nearly incredible, and nearly unintelligible, but nonetheless rigorously demonstrable fact that the square root of two is not a rational number. He was stunned by the recognition that there is something that, in Aristotle's words, "cannot be measured by even the smallest unit." Now in addition to being a mathematician, Pythagoras was the leader of a religious cult; and he was so deeply moved by his theorem—by its revelation of the mysteriously nonrational character of mathematical reality—that he ordered his followers in the cult to sacrifice a hundred oxen. The story is that, ever since then, whenever a powerful new truth is discovered, the oxen tremble.

tures of the world like those on Aristotle's list. They are more practical and, because they pertain closely to our interest in trying to manage our lives sensibly, more urgent. What presses us to inquire into them is not disinterested curiosity, or puzzlement, or wonder, or awe. It is psychic distress of another variety altogether: a kind of nagging anxiety, or unease. The difficulties we encounter in thinking about these things may sometimes, perhaps, make us dizzy. They are more likely, however, to cause us to feel troubled, restless, and dissatisfied with ourselves.

The topics to which this book is devoted have to do with the ordinary conduct of life. They pertain, in one way or another, to a question that is both ultimate and preliminary: how should a person live? Needless to say, this is not a question of only theoretical or abstract interest. It concerns us concretely, and in a very personal way. Our response to it bears directly and pervasively upon how we conduct ourselves—or, at least, upon how we propose to do so. Perhaps even more significantly, it affects how we experience our lives.

When we seek to understand the world of nature, we do so at least partly in the hope that this will enable us to live within it more comfortably. To the extent that we know our way around our environment, we feel more at home in the world. In our attempts to settle questions concerning how to live, on the other hand, what we are hoping for is the more intimate comfort of feeling at home with ourselves.

2 Philosophical issues pertaining to the question of how a person should live fall within the domain of a general theory of practical reasoning. The term "practical reasoning" refers to any of the several varieties of deliberation in which

people endeavor to decide what to do, or in which they undertake to evaluate what has been done. Among these is the particular variety of deliberation that focuses especially upon problems of *moral* evaluation. This species of practical reasoning naturally receives, from philosophers and from others as well, a great deal of attention.

It is unquestionably important for us to understand what the principles of morality require, what they endorse, and what they forbid. It goes without saying that we need to take moral considerations seriously. In my opinion, however, the importance of morality in directing our lives tends to be exaggerated. Morality is less pertinent to the shaping of our preferences and to the guidance of our conduct—it tells us less of what we need to know about what we should value and how we should live—than is commonly presumed. It is also less authoritative. Even when it does have something relevant to say, it does not necessarily have the last word. With regard to our interest in the sensible management of those aspects of our lives that are normatively significant, moral precepts are both less comprehensively germane and less definitive than we are often encouraged to believe.

People who are scrupulously moral may nonetheless be destined by deficiencies of character or of constitution to lead lives that no reasonable person would freely choose. They may have personal defects and inadequacies that have nothing much to do with morality but that make it impossible for them to live well. For example, they may be emotionally shallow; or they may lack vitality; or they may be chronically indecisive. To the extent that they do actively choose and pursue certain goals, they may devote themselves to such insipid ambitions that their experience is generally dull and without flavor. In consequence, their lives may be relentlessly banal and hollow, and—whether or not they recognize this about themselves—they may be dreadfully bored.

There are those who maintain that people who are not moral cannot be happy. Perhaps it is true that being moral is an indispensable condition for a satisfying life. It is certainly not, however, the only condition that is indispensable. Sound moral judgment is not even the only condition that is indispensable in evaluating courses of conduct. Morality can provide at most only a severely limited and insufficient answer to the question of how a person should live.

It is often presumed that the demands of morality are inherently preemptive—in other words, that they must always be accorded an overriding precedence over all other interests and claims. This strikes me as implausible. Moreover, so far as I can see, there is no very persuasive reason to believe that it is so. Morality is most particularly concerned with how our attitudes and our actions should take into account the needs, the desires, and the entitlements of other people.[4] Now why must *that* be regarded as being, without exception, the most compelling thing in our lives? To be sure, our relationships with other people are enormously important to us; and the requirements of morality to which they give rise are therefore undeniably weighty. However, it is difficult to understand why we should assume that nothing can ever, in any circum-

---

[4] There are, of course, other ways to construe the subject matter of morality. However, defining it as concerned with our relationships to others—rather than in a more Aristotelian mode, say, as concerned with the fulfillment of our essential nature—has the advantage of making especially salient what many people find to be the deepest and most difficult issue with which moral theory has to contend: namely, the seemingly inescapable possibility of conflict between the claims of morality and those of self-interest.

stances, count more heavily with us than those relationships, and that moral considerations must invariably be accepted as weightier than considerations of all other kinds.

What misleads people in this matter may be the supposition that the only alternative to accepting the requirements of morality consists in greedily permitting oneself to be driven by self-interest. Perhaps they assume that when someone is reluctant to submit his behavior to moral constraints, it must be that he is motivated by nothing more elevated than a narrow desire for some benefit to himself. This might naturally make it seem that even though there are circumstances in which morally proscribed conduct may be understandable, and maybe even forgivable, that sort of conduct can never be worthy of admiration or of genuine respect.

However, even quite reasonable and respectable people find that other things may sometimes mean more to them, and make stronger claims upon them, than *either* morality *or* themselves. There are modes of normativity that are quite properly compelling but that are grounded neither in moral nor in egoistic considerations. A person may legitimately be devoted to ideals—for instance, aesthetic, cultural, or religious ideals—whose authority for him is independent of the desiderata with which moral principles are distinctively concerned; and he may pursue these nonmoral ideals without having his own personal interests in mind at all. Although it is widely presumed that moral claims are necessarily overriding, it is far from clear that assigning a higher authority to some nonmoral mode of normativity must always be—in every circumstance and regardless of the pertinent magnitudes—a mistake.

3 Authoritative reasoning about what to do and how to behave is not limited to moral deliberation. Its scope extends, as I have suggested, to evaluations in terms of various nonmoral modes of normativity that also bear upon the conduct of life. The theory of normative practical reasoning is therefore more inclusive, with respect to the types of deliberation that it considers, than moral philosophy.

It is deeper as well. This is because it embraces issues pertaining to evaluative norms that are more comprehensive and more ultimate than the norms of morality. Morality does not really get down to the bottom of things. After all, it is not sufficient for us to recognize and to understand the moral demands that may properly be made on us. That is not enough to settle our concerns about our conduct. In addition, we need to know how much authority it is reasonable for us to accord to those demands. Morality itself cannot satisfy us about this.

There may be some individuals for whom a commitment to being morally virtuous is a categorically dominant personal ideal. Being moral is, under all conditions, more important to them than anything else. Such people will naturally accept moral requirements as unconditionally overriding. That is not, however, the only intelligible or the only appealing design for a human life. We may find that other ideals and other measures of value attract us, and that they recommend themselves to us forcefully as reasonable competitors for our controlling allegiance. Accordingly, even after we have accurately identified the commands of the moral law, there still remains—for most of us—the more fundamental practical question of just how important it is to obey them.

4 When philosophers or economists or others attempt to analyze the various structures and strategies of practical reasoning, they generally draw upon a more or less standard but nonetheless rather meager conceptual repertoire. Perhaps the most elementary as well as the most indispensable of these limited resources is the notion of what people *want*—or, synonymously (at least according to the somewhat procrustean convention that I shall adopt here), what they *desire*. This notion is rampantly ubiquitous. It is also heavily overburdened, and a bit limp. People routinely deploy it in a number of different roles, to refer to a disparate and unruly assortment of psychic conditions and events. Moreover, its various meanings are rarely distinguished; nor is there much effort to clarify how they are related. These matters are generally left carelessly undefined in the blunt usages of common sense and ordinary speech.

As a result, our understanding of various significantly problematic aspects of our lives has tended to remain partial and blurred. The standard repertoire of concepts is handy, but it does not provide adequately for the clarification of certain very important phenomena. These phenomena must be brought into sharper focus. Therefore, the usual array of conceptual resources needs to be enriched by the articulation of some additional notions. These notions, too, like the notion of desire, are both commonplace and fundamental. To an unfortunate extent, however, they have been neglected.

5 It is frequently insufficient to identify the motives that guide our conduct, or that shape our attitudes and our thinking, just by observing vaguely that there are various things we *want*. That often leaves out too much. In numerous contexts, it is both more precise and more fully explanatory to say that there is something *we care about*, or—in a phrase that I shall employ (perhaps a bit willfully) as closely equivalent to this—something *we regard as important to ourselves*. In certain cases, moreover, what moves us is an especially notable variant of caring: namely, *love*. In proposing to expand the repertoire upon which the theory of practical reason relies, these are the additional concepts that I have in mind: what we care about, what is important to us, and what we love.

There are significant relationships, of course, between wanting things and caring about them. Indeed, the notion of caring is in large part constructed out of the notion of desire. Caring about something may be, in the end, nothing more than a certain complex mode of wanting it. However, simply attributing desire to a person does not in itself convey that the person cares about the object he desires. In fact, it does not convey that the object means anything much to him at all. As everyone knows, many of our desires are utterly inconsequential. We don't really care about those desires. Satisfying them is of no importance to us whatever.

This need not be because the desires are weak. The intensity of a desire consists in its capacity to push other inclinations and interests out of the way. Sheer intensity, however, implies nothing as to whether we really care about what we want. Differences in the strengths of desires may be due to all sorts of things that are quite independent of our evaluative attitudes. They may be radically incommensurate with the relative importance to us of the desired objects.

It is true, of course, that if we happen to want something very badly, it is natural for us to care about avoiding the discomfort that we will suffer should our desire be frustrated. From our caring about *this*, however, it does not follow that we care about satisfying the desire. The reason is that it may be possible for us to avoid the frustration in another way— that is, not by obtaining the desired object but by giving up the desire instead; and that alternative may appeal to us more. People sometimes quite reasonably attempt to rid themselves entirely of certain desires, rather than to satisfy them, when they believe that satisfying the desires would be unworthy or harmful.

It will not help to augment the notion of what people want by ranking their desires in an order of preference. This is because a person who wants one thing more than another may not regard the former as being any more important to him than the latter. Suppose that someone who needs to kill a little time decides to do so by watching television, and that he chooses to watch a certain program because he prefers it to the others that are available. We cannot legitimately conclude that watching this program is something that he cares about. He watches it, after all, only to kill time. The fact that he prefers it to the others does not entail that he cares more about watching it than about watching them, because it does not entail that he cares about watching it at all.

Caring about something differs not only from wanting it, and from wanting it more than other things. It differs also from taking it to be intrinsically valuable. Even if a person believes that something has considerable intrinsic value, he may not regard it as important to himself. In attributing intrinsic value to something, we do perhaps imply that it would make sense for someone to desire it for its own sake—that is, as a final end, rather than merely as a means to something else. However, our belief that having a certain desire would not be unreasonable does not imply that we ourselves actually have the desire, nor does it imply a belief that we or anyone else ought to have it.

Something that we recognize as having intrinsic value (a life devoted to profound meditation, perhaps, or to courageous feats of knight errantry) may nevertheless fail to attract us. Moreover, it may be a matter of complete indifference to us whether anyone at all is interested in promoting or achieving it. We can easily think of many things that might well be worth having or worth doing for their own sakes, but with regard to which we consider it entirely acceptable that no one is especially drawn to them and that they are never actually pursued.

In any case, even if a person does attempt to obtain something or to do something because of its intrinsic value, it still cannot properly be inferred that he cares about it. The fact that a certain object possesses intrinsic value has to do with the *type* of value the object possesses—namely, a value that depends exclusively upon properties that inhere in the object itself rather than upon the object's relationships to other things; but it has nothing to do with *how much* value of that type the object has. What is worth having or worth doing for its own sake alone may nonetheless be worth very little. It may therefore be quite reasonable for a person to desire as final ends, entirely for the sake of their intrinsic or noninstrumental value, many things that he does not regard as being at all important to him.

For instance, there are numerous quite trivial pleasures that we seek exclusively because of their intrinsic value, but that we do not truly care about at all. When I want an ice cream cone, I want it simply for the pleasure of eating it. The pleasure is not a means to anything else; it is an end that I desire for its own sake alone. However, this hardly implies that I care about eating the ice cream. I generally recognize quite clearly on such occasions that my desire is inconsequential, and that its object is not at all important to me. A person cannot fairly be presumed to care about something, then, even if he wants it just for its own sake and thus regards fulfilling his desire for it as among his final ends.

In designing and managing their lives, people need to confront a number of significant issues. They must make up their minds concerning what they want, which things they want more than others, what they consider to be intrinsically valuable and hence appropriate for pursuit not just as a means but as a final end, and what they themselves will in fact pursue as final ends. In addition, they face a distinct further task. They have to determine what it is that they care about.

6 What, then, does it mean to care about something? It will be convenient to approach this problem indirectly. Let us begin, then, by considering what it would mean to say that we *do not really care about* going ahead with a certain plan that we have been intending to carry out.

We might say something like that to a friend who needs a favor badly, but who appears to be hesitant about asking us for it just because he is aware that doing him the favor would require us to give up our plan. The friend is embarrassed. He is reluctant to take advantage of our good nature. In fact, however, we would like to do him the favor; and we want to make it easier for him to ask. So we tell him that doing what we had been planning to do is not anything that we really care about.

When we give up going ahead with a certain plan, we may do so with either of two attitudes. On the one hand, we may give up the plan without entirely abandoning the interest and the desire that had led us to adopt it. Thus even after we decide to do the favor for our friend, carrying out our earlier intention might be something that we still want to do. Carrying out that intention has a lower priority now than it had before, but the desire to do what we had planned to do continues. Accordingly, deciding to forgo the plan entails some disappointment, or some degree of frustration. It imposes upon us, in other words, a certain cost.

On the other hand, it may be that in giving up the plan we entirely abandon our original interest in it. We lose all desire to carry it out. Then fulfilling that desire no longer occupies any position at all in the order of our priorities. We simply do not have the desire anymore. In that case, doing the favor imposes upon us no loss, and therefore no frustration or disappointment. It entails no cost of that kind. Accordingly, there is no reason for our friend to be uneasy about asking us to do him the favor and hence to give up our original plan. It is this that we might be intending to convey to him, when we tell him that we really do not care about whatever it was that we had been planning to do.

A certain caution is required here. We cannot show that a person cares about something merely by establishing that his desire for it would continue even if he should decide to forgo or to postpone satisfying that desire. The desire might be kept alive by its own intensity, after all, and not because he especially wants it to persist. Indeed, it might persist despite conscientious efforts on his part to dispel it: he might have the misfortune of being stuck with a desire that he does not want. In that case, although the desire remains alight and active within him, it does so against his own will. It does not continue because he cares about it, in other words, but only because it forces itself upon him.

When a person cares about something, on the other hand, he is willingly committed to his desire. The desire does not move him either against his will or without his endorsement. He is not its victim; nor is he passively indifferent to it. On the contrary, he himself desires that it move him. He is therefore prepared to intervene, should that be necessary, in order to ensure that it continues. If the desire tends to fade or to falter, he is disposed to refresh it and to reinforce whatever degree of influence he wishes it to exert upon his attitudes and upon his behavior.

Besides wanting to fulfill his desire, then, the person who cares about what he desires wants something else as well: he wants the desire to be sustained. Moreover, this desire for his desire to be sustained is not a merely ephemeral inclination. It is not transient or adventitious. It is a desire with which the person identifies himself, and which he accepts as expressing what he really wants.

7 Perhaps that is not all there is to caring about things. It is certainly true that caring admits of many shades and nuances that this rather limited analysis does not make explicit. But if it is at least part of a correct account, then the fact that we do actually care about various things is of fundamental significance to the character of human life.

Suppose we cared about nothing. In that case, we would do nothing to maintain any thematic unity or coherence in our desires or in the determinations of our will. We would not be actively disposed to sustain any particular interests or aims. To be sure, some degree of stable continuity might nonetheless happen to come about in our volitional lives. However, so far as our own intentions and effort are concerned, that would be just fortuitous or inadvertent. The unity and the coherence would not be the result of any purposeful initiative or guidance on our part. Various tendencies and configurations of our will would come and go; and sometimes they might last for a while. In the design of their succession and persistence, however, we ourselves would play no defining role.

Needless to say, what it is in particular that we care about has a considerable bearing upon the character and quality of our lives. It makes a great difference that certain things, and not others, are important to us. But the very fact that there *are* things that we care about—that we do care about something—is even more fundamentally significant. The reason is that this fact bears not just upon the individual specificity of a person's life, but upon its basic structure. Caring is indispensably foundational as an activity that connects and binds us to ourselves. It is through caring that we provide ourselves with volitional continuity, and in that way constitute and participate in our own agency. Regardless of how suitable or unsuitable the various things we care about may be, caring about something is essential to our being creatures of the kind that human beings are.

The ability to care requires a type of psychic complexity that may be peculiar to the members of our species. By its very nature, caring manifests and depends upon our distinctive capacity to have thoughts, desires, and attitudes that are *about* our own attitudes, desires, and thoughts. In other words, it depends upon the fact that the human mind is *reflexive*. Animals of various lesser species also have desires and attitudes. Perhaps some have thoughts as well. But animals of those species—at least, so it appears—are not self-critical. They are moved into action by impulse or by inclination, simply as it comes, without the mediation of any reflective consideration or criticism of their own motives. Insofar as they lack the capacity to form attitudes toward themselves, there is for them no possibility either of self-acceptance or of mobilizing an inner resistance to being what they are. They can neither identify with the forces that move them nor distance themselves from those forces. They are structurally incapable of such interventions in their own lives. For better or for worse, they are not equipped to take themselves seriously.

On the other hand, the self-awareness that is characteristic of human beings makes us susceptible to an inner division in which we separate from and objectify ourselves. This puts us in a position to assess the motivating forces by which we happen to be impelled, and to determine which of them to accept and which to resist. When various motivating forces within us conflict, we are generally not passive or neutral with regard to how the conflict is to be settled. We do take ourselves seriously. Accordingly, we generally enlist on one side of the conflict or on the other, and seek actively to affect the result. The actual outcome of the struggle among our own desires may therefore be for us either a victory or a defeat.

8 Creatures like ourselves are not limited to desires that move them to act. In addition, they have the reflexive capacity to form desires regarding their own desires—that is, regarding both what they want to want, and what they want not to want. These higher-order desires pertain directly

not to actions but to motives. People are commonly concerned about their motives; they want their actions to be motivated in certain ways, and not in others. Insofar as they find certain of their own motivational tendencies objectionable, they attempt to weaken and to resist them. They accept and identify with only some of the desires and dispositions that they encounter in themselves. They want to be motivated in their actions by these, and they do not want those that they consider undesirable to be effective in moving them to act.

Sometimes people are unsuccessful even in strenuously conscientious efforts to avoid being moved into action by desires that they would prefer to be motivationally ineffective. For instance, someone may act out of jealousy, or out of a desire for revenge, although he disapproves of these motives and would strongly prefer that he not be driven by them. Unhappily, as it turns out, their force is too great for him to withstand; and in the end he submits to it. Despite his resistance, the unwelcome desire is effective in moving him to act. Given that he has opposed it as well as he could, it may then reasonably be said that the desire has moved him—and that he has consequently acted—against his own will.

Sometimes, of course, the desires by which a person is motivated when he acts are desires by which he is entirely content to be moved. He may be effectively moved by a desire to be generous, for example, and this motive may be welcome to him; it may be the very desire by which, in the circumstances, he would like his conduct to be governed. In that case, when he performs the generous act, he is not only doing exactly what he wants to do, and in that sense acting freely. It is also true of him that he is desiring freely, in the parallel sense that what he is wanting as he acts—namely, to be generous—is exactly what he wants to want.

Suppose now that someone is performing an action that he wants to perform; and suppose further that his motive in performing this action is a motive by which he truly wants to be motivated. This person is in no way unwilling or indifferent either with respect to what he is doing or with respect to the desire that moves him to do it. In other words, neither the action nor the desire that motivates it is imposed upon him against his will or without his acceptance. With respect neither to the one nor to the other is he merely a passive bystander or a victim.

Under these conditions, I believe, the person is enjoying as much freedom as it is reasonable for us to desire. Indeed, it seems to me that he is enjoying as much freedom as it is possible for us to conceive. This is as close to freedom of the will as finite beings, who do not create themselves, can intelligibly hope to come.[5]

People want certain of their desires to move them into action, and they usually have certain other desires that they would prefer to remain motivationally ineffective. They are concerned about their desires in other ways as well. Thus they want some of their desires to persist; and they are indif-

---

[5] Since we do not create ourselves, there is bound to be something about us of which we ourselves are not the cause. In my opinion, the critical problem with respect to our interest in freedom is not whether the events in our volitional lives are causally determined by conditions outside ourselves. What really counts, so far as the issue of freedom goes, is not causal independence. It is autonomy. Autonomy is essentially a matter of whether we are active rather than passive in our motives and choices— whether, however we acquire them, they are the motives and choices that we really want and are therefore in no way alien to us.

ferent, or even actively opposed, to the persistence of others. These alternative possibilities—commitment to one's own desires or an absence of commitment to them—define the difference between caring and not caring. Whether a person cares or does not care about the object of his desire depends upon which of the alternatives prevails.[6]

9 There are many things that become important to us, or that become more important to us than they would otherwise be, just by virtue of the fact that we care about them. If we did not care about those things, they would either be of much less importance to us or they would be of no importance to us whatever. Consider, for instance, the people who are our friends. These people would be considerably less important to us if we had not come to care about them as much as we do. The success of a basketball team has a certain importance to its supporters, to whom its success would not be important at all if they did not happen to care about it.

Needless to say, many things are important to us despite the fact that we do not recognize that importance and therefore do not care at all about them. For instance, there are large numbers of people who have no idea that they are exposed to background radiation, and who have no idea even that there is such a thing. These people naturally do

---

[6] The inner lives of human beings are obscure, not only to others but to themselves as well. People are elusive. We tend to be rather poorly informed about our own attitudes and desires, and about where our commitments truly lie. It is useful to keep in mind, then, that a person may care about something a great deal without realizing that he cares about it. It is also possible that someone really does not care in the slightest about certain things, even though he sincerely believes that he considers those things to be extremely important to him.

not care about the level of background radiation to which they are exposed. It does not follow that the level of radiation to which they are exposed is without importance to them. It *is* important to them, whether they know anything about it or not.

However, the things that are important to a person despite the fact that he does not actually care about them, or even know about them, can have that importance to him only in virtue of standing in a certain relationship to something that he *does* care about. Suppose that someone genuinely does not care a bit about his health, or about any of the effects that radiation may produce. Suppose that he really is completely indifferent to whether the environment, or other people, or he himself, is or is not affected in those ways. In that case, the level of background radiation is not important to him. It truly does not matter to him; he has no reason to care about it. So far as he is concerned, it makes no difference whether the level is high or low. That is important only to people who care about the magnitude of the radiation either for its own sake or on account of conditions to which it may in pertinent ways be related.

If there were someone who literally cared about absolutely nothing, then nothing would be important to him.[7] He would be uninvolved in his own life: unconcerned with the coherence and continuity of his desires, neglectful of his volitional identity, and in this respect indifferent to himself. Nothing that he did or felt, and nothing that happened, would matter to him. He might *believe* that he cared about

---

[7] This leaves open the question, to which I shall respond in due course, of whether there would nonetheless be certain things that *should be* important to him and that he *should* care about.

certain things, and that those things mattered to him; however, by hypothesis, he would be wrong. Of course, he might still have various desires, and some of those desires might be stronger than others; but he would have no interest in what, from one moment to the next, his desires and preferences would be. Even if it could meaningfully be said of such a person that he had a will, it could hardly be said of him that his will was genuinely his own.

10 It is by caring about things that we infuse the world with importance. This provides us with stable ambitions and concerns; it marks our interests and our goals. The importance that our caring creates for us defines the framework of standards and aims in terms of which we endeavor to conduct our lives. A person who cares about something is guided, as his attitudes and his actions are shaped, by his continuing interest in it. Insofar as he does care about certain things, this determines how he thinks it important for him to conduct his life. The totality of the various things that a person cares about—together with his ordering of how important to him they are—effectively specifies his answer to the question of how to live.

Now suppose he wonders whether he has got it right. That is, suppose that somehow he becomes concerned about whether he really should care about the things that, as a matter of fact, he does care about. This is a concern about reasons. In raising the question of whether he should conduct his life on the basis of what he actually cares about, he is asking whether there are reasons good enough to justify him in living that way, and whether there may not be better reasons for him to live in some other way instead.

Trying to get a grip on this question might well make us even dizzier than Socrates became when he confronted the supposedly paradoxical fact that one person may become shorter than another even though his height remains the same. Indeed, once we begin asking how people *should* live, we are bound to find ourselves helplessly in a spin. The trouble is not that the question is too difficult. Asking the question tends to be disorienting, rather, because it is inescapably self-referential and leads us into an endless circle. No attempt to deal with the problem of what we have good reason to care about—to deal with it systematically and from the ground up—can possibly succeed. Efforts to conduct a rational inquiry into the matter will inevitably be defeated and turned back upon themselves.

It is not hard to see why. In order to carry out a rational evaluation of some way of living, a person must first know what evaluative criteria to employ and how to employ them. He needs to know what considerations count in favor of choosing to live in one way rather than in another, what considerations count against, and the relative weights of each. For instance, it must be clear to him how to evaluate the fact that a certain way of living leads more than others (or less than others) to personal satisfaction, to pleasure, to power, to glory, to creativity, to spiritual depth, to a harmonious relationship with the precepts of religion, to conformity with the requirements of morality, and so on.

The trouble here is a rather obvious sort of circularity. In order for a person to be able even to conceive and to initiate an inquiry into how to live, he must already have settled upon the judgments at which the inquiry aims. Identifying the question of how one should live—that is, understanding just what question it is and just how to go about answering it—requires that one specify the criteria that are to be employed in evaluating various ways of living. Identifying the question is, indeed, tantamount to specifying those criteria: what the question asks is, precisely, what way of living best satisfies them. But identifying the criteria to be employed in evaluating various ways of living is also tantamount to providing an answer to the question of how to live, for the answer to this question is simply that one should live in the way that best satisfies whatever criteria are to be employed for evaluating lives.

Clarifying what question the inquiry is to explore consists in identifying the criteria on the basis of which the exploration is to be pursued. But this comes to the same thing as affirming the judgments concerning what makes one life preferable to another, at which the inquiry aims. One might say, then, that the question is *systematically inchoate.* It is impossible to identify the question exactly, or to see how to go about inquiring into it, until the answer to the question is known.

Here is another way to bring out the difficulty. Something is important to a person only in virtue of a difference that it makes. If everything would be exactly the same with that thing as without it, then it makes no sense for anyone to care about it. It cannot really be of any importance. Of course, it cannot be enough for it merely to make *some* difference. After all, everything does make some difference; but not everything is important. If something is to be important, obviously, the difference that it makes cannot be utterly inconsequential. It cannot be so trivial that it would be reasonable to ignore it entirely. In other words, it must be a difference of some importance. In order for a person to know how to determine what is important to himself, then, he must already know how to identify certain things as making differences that are important to him. Formulating a criterion of importance presupposes possession of the very criterion that is to be formulated. The circularity is both inescapable and fatal.

11 There can be no well-ordered inquiry into the question of how one has reason to live, because the prior question of how to identify and to evaluate the reasons that are pertinent in deciding how one should live cannot be settled until it has first been settled how one should live. The question of what one should care about must already be answered, in other words, before a rationally conducted inquiry aimed at answering it can even get under way. It is true, of course, that once a person has identified *some* things as important to him, he may readily be able on that basis to identify others. The fact that he cares about certain things will very likely make it possible for him to recognize that it would be reasonable for him to care about various related things as well. What is *not* possible is for a person who does not already care at least about *something* to discover reasons for caring about anything. Nobody can pull himself up by his own bootstraps.

This means that the most basic and essential question for a person to raise concerning the conduct of his life cannot be the *normative* question of how he *should* live. That question can sensibly be asked only on the basis of a prior answer to the *factual* question of what he actually *does* care about. If he cares about nothing, he cannot even begin to inquire methodically into how he should live; for his caring about nothing entails that there is nothing that can count with him as a reason in favor of living in one way rather than in another. In that case, to be sure, the fact that he is unable to determine how he should live may not cause him any distress. After all, if there really is nothing that he considers important to him, he will not consider *that* to be important to him either.

As a matter of fact, however, nearly everyone does care about something. Nearly everyone cares about staying alive, for instance, and about avoiding severe injury, disease, hunger, and various modes of psychic distress and disorder; they care about their children, about their livelihoods, and about how others think of them. Needless to say, they generally also care about many other things as well. For nearly everyone, there are a number of considerations that count as reasons for preferring one way of living over another.

Moreover, a number of the considerations that count as reasons for these preferences are the same for nearly everyone. This is not a coincidence, nor is it an artifact of some rather special set of historical or cultural conditions. People care about many of the same things because the natures of human beings, and the basic conditions of human life, are grounded in biological, psychological, and environmental facts that are not subject to very much variation or change.[8]

Nevertheless, it may easily seem that an empirical account of what people actually care about and consider important to themselves—even if all those things were to be entirely the same and in the same order for everyone—would miss the whole point of our original concern with the problem of what sort of life one should live. How could a purely factual account like that even diminish, much less definitively allay, our initial disturbing uncertainty about how to conduct our

---

[8] People do differ quite a bit, of course, in their orderings. Although many things are important to nearly everyone, people's preferences and priorities among the things they all care about are by no means the same.

lives? Merely knowing how things are, it would seem, does nothing to justify them. Why should the fact that people generally employ certain criteria in evaluating alternatives—or that they always do so—be considered sufficient to establish that those are the criteria it is most reasonable to employ? Becoming aware of the status quo hardly appears to give us, in itself, a good enough reason for accepting it.

We need to understand, however, that the ambition to provide an exhaustively rational warrant for the way in which we are to conduct our lives is misconceived. The pan-rationalist fantasy of demonstrating—from the ground up—how we have most reason to live is incoherent and must be abandoned. It is not the factual question about caring that misses the point, but the normative one. If we are to resolve our difficulties and hesitations in settling upon a way to live, what we need most fundamentally is not reasons or proofs. It is clarity and confidence. Coping with our troubled and restless uncertainty about how to live does not require us to discover what way of living can be justified by definitive argument. Rather, it requires us simply to understand what it is that we ourselves really care about, and to be decisively and robustly confident in caring about it.[9]

12 The degree to which confidence in our beliefs or attitudes or ways of behaving is warranted often depends quite properly upon the strength of the reasons by

---

[9] Being confident must not be confused with being fanatical, or with having a closed mind. Even the most decisively and robustly confident person may be capable of recognizing that additional evidence or experience might come along that would lead him to change his attitudes or his beliefs. His confidence may imply that he considers such a change to be unlikely, but it does not mean that he is determined to prevent it.

which the confidence is supported. In certain matters, however, it would be foolishly misguided to insist that confidence is appropriate only to the extent that it is securely grounded in reasons. For instance, normal people are as a rule not at all uncertain concerning whether to care about their own survival, or about the well-being of their children. We care about such things without inhibition or reserve, and without any anxiety concerning whether it can be shown to be proper for us to do so.[10] We do not suppose that the sturdy confidence that typically characterizes our attitudes regarding them actually depends—nor do we suppose that it should depend—upon a conviction that the confidence can be vindicated by rationally compelling arguments.

Perhaps there are such arguments, but that is not to the point. The fact that people ordinarily do not hesitate in their commitments to the continuation of their lives, and to the well-being of their children, does not derive from any actual consideration by them of reasons; nor does it depend even upon an assumption that good reasons could be found. Those commitments are innate in us. They are not based upon deliberation. They are not responses to any commands of rationality.

The commands to which they do in fact respond are grounded in a source that is constituted not by judgments and reasons, but by a particular mode of caring about things. They are commands of love. The basis for our confidence in caring about our children and our lives is that, in virtue of necessities

---

[10] To be sure, we may be uncertain concerning how much to care, or concerning whether to care more about one thing or about another. We are nonetheless quite confident that our lives and our children are important to us, even though we may not know exactly how important to us we want them to be.

that are biologically embedded in our nature, we love our children and we love living. We generally continue to love them, indeed, even when they disappoint us or when they bring us suffering. Often we go on loving them even after we have become persuaded that the love is unreasonable.[11]

People do not all love the same things. The fact that I love my life and my children does not mean that I love yours. Moreover, there are likely to be some people who genuinely and wholeheartedly love what we ourselves fear or despise. That presents a problem. It should not be assumed, however, that we cannot deal sensibly and effectively with this problem except by marshaling evidence and arguments. In fact, we really do not need to decide who is right.

The problem for us is to protect our children and our lives. One way to accomplish this, of course, would be by persuading our opponents that they are wrong. But we surely cannot count on being able, by neutral and universally acceptable rational methods, to make a convincing case that they have made a mistake. This does not imply that it must therefore be unreasonable for us to defend what we love against those by whom it is threatened, or that we cannot be justified in promoting its interests despite the resistance or indifference of those to whom it does not appeal.

We do not consider parents to be acting unreasonably or unjustifiably if they continue to love and to protect their chil-

---

[11] Of course, it is possible for our readiness to obey the commands of love to be undermined by experiences or by thoughts that we regard as giving us reasons to care less about our children or about our lives. Some people do turn against their children, after all, and some do choose to end their lives. The fact that they think they have good reasons to stop loving life or to stop loving their children does not mean that it was reason that accounted for or that warranted the love while it lasted.

dren with unshaken confidence and devotion even after discovering that their children are regarded by others with distaste or contempt. Nor are parents generally condemned for doing this even when they are utterly incapable of arguing plausibly, much less of proving, that the hostility to their children is unwarranted. We do not think that a person is being irrationally stubborn, or that his behavior is reprehensibly arbitrary, if he insists upon defending his own life even when he cannot refute the complaints against him of those who wish that he were dead.

Why should we be any more embarrassed by the impossibility of mobilizing rigorously demonstrative justifications of our moral ideals, or of the compelling importance to us of other things that we love? Why should the unavailability of decisive supporting reasons disturb our confidence in the vision of life that is defined by what we care about, or inhibit our readiness to oppose those whose vision of what is important threatens our own? Why should we not be happy to fight for what we wholeheartedly love, even when there are no good arguments to show that it is correct for us to love it rather than to love other things instead?

13 So far I have characterized what I refer to as "love" only as a particular mode of caring. In the next chapter, I will attempt to explain more fully what I have in mind. The category of love is, of course, notoriously difficult to elucidate.[12] My task will be relatively manageable, however, since I will not endeavor to provide anything like a compre-

---

[12] The prospect of undertaking to identify it with some precision makes me think of a rather unsettling bit of advice that I understand was offered by Niels Bohr. He is said to have cautioned that one should never speak more clearly than one can think.

hensive analytical account of the diverse and complex range of conditions to which the term "love" is customarily made to refer. My own usage of the term coincides with part of that range but is not designed to coincide with all of it. Thus I need to define only the more limited set of phenomena that is especially germane to my discussion. Certain features that are salient in various other conditions that are familiarly called "love," and that may even be definitive of those conditions, are inessential to these phenomena. Therefore, they are not included in my account.

Two

On Love, and Its Reasons

1 There has recently been quite a bit of interest among philosophers in issues concerning whether our conduct must invariably be guided strictly by universal moral principles, which we apply impartially in all situations, or whether favoritism of one sort or another may sometimes be reasonable. In fact, we do not always feel that it is necessary or important for us to be meticulously evenhanded. The situation strikes us differently when our children, or our countries, or our most cherished personal ambitions are at stake. We commonly think that it is appropriate, and perhaps even obligatory, to favor certain people over others who may be just as worthy but with whom our relationships are more distant. Similarly, we often consider ourselves entitled to prefer investing our resources in projects to which we happen to be especially devoted, instead of in others that we may readily acknowledge to have somewhat greater inherent merit. The problem with which philosophers have been concerned is not so much to determine whether preferences of this kind are ever legitimate. Rather, it is to explain under what conditions and in what way they may be justified.

An example that has been widely discussed in this connection has to do with a man who sees two people on the verge of drowning, who can save only one, and who must decide which of the two he will try to save. One of them is a person whom he does not know. The other is his wife. It is hard to think, of course, that the man should make up his mind by just tossing a coin. We are strongly inclined to believe that it would be far more appropriate for him, in a situation like this one, to put aside considerations of impartiality or fairness altogether. Surely the man should rescue his wife. But what is his warrant for treating the two endangered people so unequally? What acceptable principle can the man invoke that would legitimate his decision to let the stranger drown?

One of the most interesting contemporary philosophers, Bernard Williams, suggests that the man already goes wrong if he thinks it is incumbent upon him even to look for a principle from which he could infer that, in circumstances like those in which he finds himself, it is permissible to save one's wife. Instead, Williams says, "it might . . . [be] hoped . . . that his motivating thought, fully spelled out, would be [just] the thought that it was his wife." If he adds to this the further thought that in situations of this kind it is *permissible* to save one's wife, Williams admonishes that the man is having "one thought too many." In other words, there is something fishy about the whole notion that when his wife is drowning, the man needs to rely upon some general rule from which a reason that justifies his decision to save her can be derived.[1]

2 I am very sympathetic to Williams's line of thought.[2] However, the example as he presents it is significantly out of focus. It cannot work in the way that he intends, if what it stipulates concerning one of the drowning people is merely that she is the man's wife. After all, suppose that for quite good reasons the man detests and fears his wife. Sup-

---

[1] Bernard Williams, "Persons, Character and Morality," in his *Moral Luck* (Cambridge University Press, 1981), 18.

[2] I do have problems with a couple of the details. For one thing, I cannot help wondering why the man should have even the one thought that it's his wife. Are we supposed to imagine that at first he didn't recognize her? Or are we supposed to imagine that at first he didn't remember that they were married, and had to remind himself of that? It seems to me that the strictly correct number of thoughts for this man is zero. Surely the normal thing is that he sees what's happening in the water, and he jumps in to save his wife. Without thinking at all. In the circumstances that the example describes, any thought whatever is one thought too many.

pose that she detests him too, and that she has recently en-
gaged in several viciously determined attempts to murder
him. Or suppose that it was nothing but a cold-bloodedly
arranged marriage of convenience anyhow, and that they
have never even been in the same room together except dur-
ing a perfunctory two-minute wedding ceremony thirty
years ago. Surely, to specify nothing more than a bare legal
relationship between the man and the drowning woman
misses the point.

Let us put aside the matter of their civil status, then, and
stipulate instead that the man in the example *loves* one (and
not the other) of the two people who are drowning. In that
case, it certainly would be incongruous for him to look for a
reason to save her. If he does truly love her, then he necessarily already has that reason. It is simply that she is in trouble
and needs his help. Just in itself, the fact that he loves her
entails that he takes her distress as a more powerful reason
for going to her aid than for going to the aid of someone
about whom he knows nothing. The need of his beloved for
help provides him with this reason, without requiring that
he think of any additional considerations and without the
interposition of any general rules.

To take such things into account would indeed be to have
one thought too many. If the man does not recognize the
distress of the woman he loves as a reason for saving her
rather than the stranger, then he does not genuinely love her
at all. Loving someone or something essentially *means* or
consists in, among other things, taking its interests as reasons
for acting to serve those interests. Love is itself, for the lover,
a source of reasons. It creates the reasons by which his acts
of loving concern and devotion are inspired.[3]

---

[3] That, precisely, is how love makes the world go 'round.

3 Love is often understood as being, most basically, a response to the perceived worth of the beloved. We are moved to love something, on this account, by an appreciation of what we take to be its exceptional inherent value. The appeal of that value is what captivates us and turns us into lovers. We begin loving the things that we love because we are struck by their value, and we continue to love them for the sake of their value. If we did not find the beloved valuable, we would not love it.

This may well fit certain cases of what would commonly be identified as love. However, the sort of phenomenon that I have in mind when referring here to love is essentially something else. As I am construing it, love is not necessarily a response grounded in awareness of the inherent value of its object. It may sometimes arise like that, but it need not do so. Love may be brought about—in ways that are poorly understood—by a disparate variety of natural causes. It is entirely possible for a person to be caused to love something without noticing its value, or without being at all impressed by its value, or despite recognizing that there really is nothing especially valuable about it. It is even possible for a person to come to love something despite recognizing that its inherent nature is actually and utterly bad. That sort of love is doubtless a misfortune. Still, such things happen.

It is true that the beloved invariably *is*, indeed, valuable to the lover. However, perceiving that value is not at all an indispensable *formative* or *grounding* condition of the love. It need not be a perception of value in what he loves that moves the lover to love it. The truly essential relationship between love and the value of the beloved goes in the opposite direction. It is not necessarily as a *result* of recognizing their value and of being captivated by it that we love things.

Rather, what we love necessarily *acquires* value for us *because* we love it. The lover does invariably and necessarily perceive the beloved as valuable, but the value he sees it to possess is a value that derives from and that depends upon his love. Consider the love of parents for their children. I can declare with unequivocal confidence that I do not love my children because I am aware of some value that inheres in them independent of my love for them. The fact is that I loved them even before they were born—before I had any especially relevant information about their personal characteristics or their particular merits and virtues. Furthermore, I do not believe that the valuable qualities they do happen to possess, strictly in their own rights, would really provide me with a very compelling basis for regarding them as having greater worth than many other possible objects of love that in fact I love much less. It is quite clear to me that I do not love them more than other children because I believe they are better.

At times, we speak of people or of other things as "unworthy" of our love. Perhaps this means that the cost of loving them would be greater than the benefit of doing so; or perhaps it means that to love those things would be in some way demeaning. In any case, if I ask myself whether my children are worthy of my love, my emphatic inclination is to reject the question as misguided. This is not because it goes so clearly without saying that my children *are* worthy. It is because my love for them is not at all a response to an evaluation either of them or of the consequences for me of loving them. If my children should turn out to be ferociously wicked, or if it should become apparent that loving them somehow threatened my hope of leading a decent life, I might perhaps recognize that my love for them was regrettable. But I suspect that after coming finally to acknowledge this, I would continue to love them anyhow.

It is not because I have noticed their value, then, that I love my children as I do. Of course, I do perceive them to have value; so far as I am concerned, indeed, their value is beyond measure. That, however, is not the basis of my love. It is really the other way around. The particular value that I attribute to my children is not inherent in them but depends upon my love for them. The reason they are so precious to me is simply that I love them so much. As for why it is that human beings do tend generally to love their children, the explanation presumably lies in the evolutionary pressures of natural selection. In any case, it is plainly *on account of* my love for them that they have acquired in my eyes a value that otherwise they would certainly not possess.

This relationship between love and the value of the be-loved—namely, that love is not necessarily grounded in the value of the beloved but does necessarily make the beloved valuable to the lover—holds not only for parental love but quite generally.[4] Most profoundly, perhaps, it is love that accounts for the value to us of life itself. Our lives normally

---

[4] There are certain objects of love—certain ideals, for instance—that do appear in many instances to be loved on account of their value. However, it is not necessary that the love of an ideal originate or be grounded in that way. A person might come to love justice or truth or moral rectitude quite blindly, after all, merely as a result of having been brought up to do so. Moreover, it is generally not considerations of value that account for the fact that a person comes to be selflessly devoted to one ideal or value rather than to some other. What leads people to care more about truth than about justice, or more about beauty than about morality, or more about one religion than about another, is generally not some prior appreciation that what they love more has greater inherent value than what they care about less.

have for us a value that we accept as commandingly authoritative. Moreover, the value to us of living radiates pervasively. It radically conditions the value that we attribute to many other things. It is a powerful—indeed, a comprehensively foundational—generator of value. There are innumerable things that we care about a great deal, and that therefore are very important to us, just because of the ways in which they bear upon our interest in survival.

Why do we so naturally, and with such unquestioning assurance, take self-preservation to be an incomparably compelling and legitimate reason for pursuing certain courses of action? We certainly do not assign this overwhelming importance to staying alive because we believe that there is some great value inherent in our lives, or in what we are doing with them—a value that is independent of our own attitudes and dispositions. Even when we think rather well of ourselves, and suppose that our lives may actually be valuable in such a way, that is not normally why we are so determined to hang on to them. We take the fact that some course of action would contribute to our survival as a reason for pursuing it just because, presumably again thanks to natural selection, we are innately constituted to love living.

4 Let me now attempt to explain what I have in mind when I speak here of love.

The object of love is often a concrete individual: for instance, a person or a country. It may also be something more abstract: for instance, a tradition, or some moral or nonmoral ideal. There will frequently be greater emotional color and urgency in love when the beloved is an individual than when it is something like social justice, or scientific truth, or the way a certain family or a certain cultural group does things; but that is not always the case. In any event, it is not among the defining features of love that it must be hot rather than cool.

One distinctive feature of loving has to do with the particular status of the value that is accorded to its objects. Insofar as we care about something at all, we regard it as important to ourselves; but we may consider it to have that importance only because we regard it as a means to something else. When we love something, however, we go further. We care about it not as merely a means, but as an end. It is in the nature of loving that we consider its objects to be valuable in themselves and to be important to us for their own sakes.

Love is, most centrally, a *disinterested* concern for the existence of what is loved, and for what is good for it. The lover desires that his beloved flourish and not be harmed; and he does not desire this just for the sake of promoting some other goal. Someone might care about social justice only because it reduces the likelihood of rioting; and someone might care about the health of another person just because she cannot be useful to him unless she is in good shape. For the lover, the condition of his beloved is important in itself, apart from any bearing that it may have on other matters.

Love may involve strong feelings of attraction, which the lover supports and rationalizes with flattering descriptions of the beloved. Moreover, lovers often enjoy the company of their beloveds, cherish various types of intimate connection with them, and yearn for reciprocity. These enthusiasms are not essential. Nor is it essential that a person like what he loves. He may even find it distasteful. As in other modes of caring, the heart of the matter is neither affective nor cognitive. It is volitional. Loving something has less to do with what a person believes, or with how he feels, than with a configuration of the will that consists in a practical concern for what is good for the beloved. This volitional configuration shapes the dispositions and conduct of the lover with respect to what he loves, by guiding him in the design and ordering of his relevant purposes and priorities.

It is important to avoid confusing love—as circumscribed by the concept that I am defining—with infatuation, lust, obsession, possessiveness, and dependency in their various forms. In particular, relationships that are primarily romantic or sexual do not provide very authentic or illuminating paradigms of love as I am construing it. Relationships of those kinds typically include a number of vividly distracting elements, which do not belong to the essential nature of love as a mode of disinterested concern, but that are so confusing that they make it nearly impossible for anyone to be clear about just what is going on. Among relationships between humans, the love of parents for their infants or small children is the species of caring that comes closest to offering recognizably pure instances of love.

There is a certain variety of concern for others that may also be entirely disinterested, but that differs from love because it is impersonal. Someone who is devoted to helping the sick or the poor for their own sakes may be quite indifferent to the particularity of those whom he seeks to help. What qualifies people to be beneficiaries of his charitable concern is not that he loves them. His generosity is not a response to their identities as individuals; it is not aroused by their personal characteristics. It is induced merely by the fact that he regards them as members of a relevant class. For someone who is eager to help the sick or the poor, any sick or poor person will do.

When it comes to what we love, on the other hand, that sort of indifference to the specificity of the object is out of the question. The significance to the lover of what he loves is not that his beloved is an instance or an exemplar. Its importance to him is not generic; it is ineluctably particular. For a person who wants simply to help the sick or the poor, it would make perfectly good sense to choose his beneficiaries randomly from among those who are sick or poor enough to qualify. It does not matter who in particular the needy persons are. Since he does not really care about any of them as such, they are entirely acceptable substitutes for each other. The situation of a lover is very different. There can be no equivalent substitute for his beloved. It might really be all the same to someone moved by charity whether he helps this needy person or that one. It cannot possibly be all the same to the lover whether he is devoting himself disinterestedly to what he actually does love or—no matter how similar it might be—to something else instead.

Finally, it is a necessary feature of love that it is not under our direct and immediate voluntary control. What a person cares about, and how much he cares about it, may under certain conditions be up to him. It may at times be possible for him to bring it about that he cares about something, or that he does not care about it, just by making up his mind one way or the other. Whether the requirements of protecting and supporting that thing provide him with acceptable reasons for acting, and how weighty those reasons are, depends in cases like that upon what he himself decides. With regard to certain things, however, a person may discover that he cannot affect whether or how much he cares about them merely by his own decision. The issue is not up to him at all.

For instance, under normal conditions people cannot help caring quite a bit about staying alive, about remaining physically intact, about not being radically isolated, about avoiding chronic frustration, and so on. They really have no choice. Canvassing reasons and making judgments and decisions will not change anything. Even if they should consider it a good idea to stop caring about whether they have any contact with other human beings, or about fulfilling their ambitions, or about their lives and their limbs, they would be unable to stop. They would find that, whatever they thought or decided, they were still disposed to protect themselves from extreme physical and psychic deprivation and harm. In matters like these, we are subject to a necessity that forcefully constrains the will and that we cannot elude merely by choosing or deciding to do so.[5]

The necessity by which a person is bound in cases like these is not a cognitive necessity, generated by the require-

---

[5] If someone under ordinary conditions cared nothing at all about dying or being mutilated, or about being deprived of all human contact, we would not regard him merely as atypical. We would consider him to be deranged. There is no strictly logical flaw in those attitudes, but they count nonetheless as irrational—i.e., as violating a defining condition of humanity. There is a sense of rationality that has very little to do with consistency or with other formal considerations. Thus suppose that a person deliberately causes death or deep suffering for no reason, or (Hume's example) seeks the destruction of a multitude in order to avoid a minor injury to one of his fingers. Anyone who could bring himself to do such things would naturally be regarded—despite his having made no logical error—as "crazy." He would be regarded, in other words, as lacking reason. We are accustomed to understanding rationality as precluding contradiction and incoherence—as limiting what it is possible for us to think. There is also a sense of rationality in which it limits what we can bring ourselves to do or to accept. In the one sense, the alternative to reason is what we recognize as inconceivable. In the other, it is what we find unthinkable.

ments of reason. The way in which it makes alternatives un-
available is not by limiting, as logical necessities do, the possibilities of coherent thought. When we understand that a
proposition is self-contradictory, it is impossible for us to
believe it; similarly, we cannot help accepting a proposition
when we understand that to deny it would be to embrace a
contradiction. What people cannot help caring about, on the
other hand, is not mandated by logic. It is not primarily a
constraint upon belief. It is a volitional necessity, which consists essentially in a limitation of the will.

There are certain things that people cannot do, despite
possessing the relevant natural capacities or skills, because
they cannot muster the will to do them. Loving is circumscribed by a necessity of that kind: what we love and what
we fail to love is not up to us. Now the necessity that is
characteristic of love does not constrain the movements of
the will through an imperious surge of passion or compulsion
by which the will is defeated and subdued. On the contrary,
the constraint operates from within our own will itself. It is
by our own will, and not by any external or alien force, that
we are constrained. Someone who is bound by volitional necessity is unable to form a determined and effective intention—regardless of what motives and reasons he may have
for doing so—to perform (or to refrain from performing) the
action that is at issue. If he undertakes an attempt to perform
it, he discovers that he simply cannot bring himself to carry
the attempt all the way through.

Love comes in degrees. We love some things more than
we love others. Accordingly, the necessity that love imposes
on the will is rarely absolute. We may love something and
yet be willing to harm it, in order to protect something else
for which our love is greater. A person may well find it possi-

ble under certain conditions, then, to perform an act that under others he could not bring himself to perform. For instance, the fact that a person sacrifices his life when he believes that doing so will save his country from catastrophic harm does not reveal thereby that he does not love living; nor does his sacrifice show that he could also have brought himself to accept death willingly when he believed that there was less to be gained. Even of people who commit suicide because they are miserable, it is generally true that they love living. What they would really like, after all, would be to give up not their lives but their misery.

5 There is among philosophers a recurrent hope that there are certain final ends whose unconditional adoption might be shown to be in some way a requirement of reason. But this is a will-o'-the-wisp.[6] There are no necessities of logic or of rationality that dictate what we are to love. What we love is shaped by the universal exigencies of human life, together with those other needs and interests that derive more particularly from the features of individual character and experience. Whether something is to be an object of

---

[6] Some philosophers believe that the ultimate warrant for moral principles is to be found in reason. In their view, moral precepts are inescapably authoritative precisely because they articulate conditions of rationality itself. This cannot be correct. The sort of opprobrium that attaches to moral transgressions is quite unlike the sort of opprobrium that attaches to violations of the requirements of reason. Our response to people who behave immorally is not at all the same as our response to people whose thinking is illogical. Manifestly, there is something other than the importance of being rational that supports the injunction to be moral. For a discussion of this point, cf. my "Rationalism in Ethics," in *Autonomes Handeln: Beiträge zur Philosophie von Harry G. Frankfurt*, ed. M. Betzler and B. Guckes (Akademie Verlag, 2000).

our love cannot be decisively evaluated either by any a priori method or through examination of just its inherent properties. It can be measured only against requirements that are imposed upon us by other things that we love. In the end, these are determined for us by biological and other natural conditions, concerning which we have nothing much to say.[7]

The origins of normativity do not lie, then, either in the transient incitements of personal feeling and desire, or in the severely anonymous requirements of eternal reason. They lie in the contingent necessities of love. These move us, as feelings and desires do; but the motivations that love engenders are not merely adventitious or (to use Kant's term) heteronomous. Rather, like the universal laws of pure reason, they express something that belongs to our most intimate and most fundamental nature. Unlike the necessities of reason, however, those of love are not impersonal. They are constituted by and embedded in structures of the will through which the specific identity of the individual is most particularly defined.

Of course, love is often unstable. Like any natural condition, it is vulnerable to circumstance. Alternatives are always conceivable, and some of them may be attractive. It is generally possible for us to imagine ourselves loving things other than those that we do love, and to wonder whether that might not be in some way preferable. The possibility that there may be superior alternatives does not imply, however,

---

[7] It may be perfectly reasonable to insist that people *should* care about certain things, which they do not actually care about, but only if something is known about what they *do* in fact care about. If we may assume that people care about leading secure and satisfying lives, for example, we will be justified in trying to see to it that they care about things that we believe are indispensable for achieving security and satisfaction. It is in this way that a "rational" basis for morality may be developed.

that our behavior is irresponsibly arbitrary when we whole-heartedly adopt and pursue the final ends that our loving actually sets for us. Those ends are not fixed by shallow impulse, or by gratuitous stipulation; nor are they determined by what we merely happen at one time or another to find appealing or to decide that we want. The volitional necessity that constrains us in what we love may be as rigorously unyielding to personal inclination or choice as the more austere necessities of reason. What we love is not up to us. We cannot help it that the direction of our practical reasoning is in fact governed by the specific final ends that our love has defined for us. We cannot fairly be charged with reprehensible arbitrariness, nor with a willful or negligent lack of objectivity, since these things are not under our immediate control at all.

To be sure, it may at times be within our power to control them indirectly. We are sometimes capable of bringing about conditions that would cause us to stop loving what we love, or to love other things. But suppose that our love is so wholehearted, and that we are so satisfied to be in its grip, that we could not bring ourselves to alter it even if measures by which it could be altered were available. In that case, the alternative is not a genuine option. Whether it would be better for us to love differently is a question that we are unable to take seriously. For us, as a practical matter, the issue cannot effectively arise.

6 In the end, our readiness to be satisfied with loving what we actually do love does not rest upon the reliability of arguments or of evidence. It rests upon confidence in ourselves. This is not a matter of being satisfied with the range and reliability of our cognitive faculties, or of believing that our information is sufficient. It is confidence of a more fun-

damental and personal variety. What ensures that we accept
our love without equivocation, and what thereby secures the
stability of our final ends, is that we have confidence in the
controlling tendencies and responses of our own volitional
character.

It is by these nonvoluntary tendencies and responses of
our will that love is constituted and that loving moves us. It
is by these same configurations of the will, moreover, that
our individual identities are most fully expressed and defined. The necessities of a person's will guide and limit his
agency. They determine what he may be willing to do, what
he cannot help doing, and what he cannot bring himself to
do. They determine as well what he may be willing to accept
as a reason for acting, what he cannot help considering to be
a reason for acting, and what he cannot bring himself to
count as a reason for acting. In these ways, they set the
boundaries of his practical life; and thus they fix his shape
as an active being. Any anxiety or uneasiness that he comes
to feel on account of recognizing what he is constrained to
love goes to the heart, then, of his attitude toward his own
character as a person. That sort of disturbance is symptom-
atic of a lack of confidence in what he himself is.

The psychic integrity in which self-confidence consists
can be ruptured by the pressure of unresolved discrepancies
and conflicts among the various things that we love. Disor-
ders of that sort undermine the unity of the will and put us
at odds with ourselves. The opposition within the scope of
what we love means that we are subject to requirements that
are both unconditional and incompatible. That makes it impossible for us to plot a steady volitional course. If our love
of one thing clashes unavoidably with our love of another,
we may well find it impossible to accept ourselves as we are.

However, it may sometimes happen that there is in fact no conflict among the motivations that our various loves impose upon us, and hence that there is no source or locus within us of opposition to any of them. In that case, we have no basis for any uncertainty or reluctance in acceding to the motivations that our loving engenders. Nothing else that we care about as much, or that is of comparable importance to us, provides a ground for hesitation or doubt. Accordingly, we would be able deliberately to arouse ourselves to resist the requirements of love only by resorting to some contrived ad hoc maneuver. That *would* be arbitrary. On the other hand, it cannot be improperly arbitrary for a person to accept the impetus of a love concerning which he is well informed, and that is coherent with the other demands of his will, for he has no pertinent basis for declining to do so.

7 What we love is necessarily important to us, just because we love it. There is also a rather different point to be made here. Loving itself is important to us. Quite apart from our particular interest in the various things that we love, we have a more generic and an even more fundamental interest in loving as such.

A clear and familiar illustration of this is provided by parental love. Besides the fact that *my children* are important to me for their own sakes, there is the additional fact that *loving my children* is important to me for *its* own sake. Whatever burdens and distresses loving them may in the course of time have brought me, my life was notably altered and enhanced when I came to love them. One thing that leads people to have children is precisely the expectation that it will enrich their lives, and that it will do this simply by giving them more to love.

Why is loving so important to us? Why is a life in which a person loves something, regardless of what it is, better for him—assuming, of course, that other things are more or less equal—than a life in which there is nothing that he loves? Part of the explanation has to do with the importance to us of having final ends. We need goals that we consider to be worth attaining for their own sake and not only for the sake of other things.

Insofar as we care about anything, we make various things important to us—namely, the things that we care about, together with whatever may be indispensable as a means to them. This provides us with aims and ambitions, thereby making it possible for us to formulate courses of action that are not entirely pointless. It enables us, in other words, to conceive activity that is meaningful in the rather minimal sense that it has some purpose. However, activity that is meaningful only in this very limited sense cannot be fully satisfying. It cannot even be fully intelligible to us.

Aristotle observes that desire is "empty and vain" unless "there is some end of the things we do which we desire for its own sake."[8] It is not enough for us to see merely that it is important for us to attain a certain end because that will facilitate our attaining some further end. We cannot make sense of what we are doing if none of our goals has any importance except in virtue of enabling us to reach other goals. There must be "some end of the things we do which we desire for its own sake." Otherwise our activity, regardless of how purposeful it may be, will have no real point. We can

---

[8] *Nicomachean Ethics* 1094a18–21. Aristotle apparently believed that there must be a single final end at which everything we do aims. I mean to endorse only the more modest view that each of the things we do must aim at some final end.

never be genuinely satisfied by it, because it will always be unfinished. Since what it aims at is always a preliminary or a preparation, it will leave us always short of completion. The actions we perform will truly seem empty and vain to us, and we will tend to lose interest in what we do.

8 It is an interesting question why a life in which activity is locally purposeful but nonetheless fundamentally aimless—having an immediate goal but no final end—should be considered undesirable. What would necessarily be so terrible about a life that is empty of meaning in this sense? The answer is, I think, that without final ends we would find nothing truly important either as an end or as a means. The importance to us of everything would depend upon the importance to us of something else. We would not really care about anything unequivocally and without conditions.

Insofar as this became clear to us, we would recognize our volitional tendencies and dispositions as pervasively inconclusive. It would then become impossible for us to involve ourselves conscientiously and responsibly in managing the course of our intentions and decisions. We would have no settled interest in designing or in sustaining any particular continuity in the configurations of our will. A major aspect of our reflective connection to ourselves, in which our distinctive character as human beings lies, would thus be severed. Our lives would be passive, fragmented, and thereby drastically impaired. Even if we might perhaps continue to maintain some meager vestige of active self-awareness, we would be dreadfully bored.

Boredom is a serious matter. It is not a condition that we seek to avoid just because we do not find it enjoyable. In fact, the avoidance of boredom is a profound and compelling human need. Our aversion to being bored has considerably greater significance than a mere reluctance to experience a state of consciousness that is more or less unpleasant. The aversion arises out of our sensitivity to a far more portentous threat.

The essence of boredom is that we have no interest in what is going on. We do not care about any of it; none of it is important to us. As a natural consequence of this, our motivation to stay focused weakens; and we undergo a corresponding attenuation of psychic vitality. In its most characteristic and familiar manifestations, being bored involves a radical reduction in the sharpness and steadiness of attention. The level of our mental energy and activity diminishes. Our responsiveness to ordinary stimuli flattens out and shrinks. Within the scope of our awareness, differences are not noticed and distinctions are not made. Thus our conscious field becomes more and more homogeneous. As the boredom expands and becomes increasingly dominant, it entails a progressive diminution of significant differentiation within consciousness.

At the limit, when the field of consciousness has become totally undifferentiated, there is an end to all psychic movement or change. The complete homogenization of consciousness is tantamount to a cessation of conscious experience entirely. In other words, when we are bored we tend to fall asleep.

Any substantial increase in the extent to which we are bored threatens the very continuation of conscious mental life. What our preference for avoiding boredom manifests is therefore not merely a casual resistance to more or less innocuous discomfort. It expresses a quite primitive urge for psychic survival. I think it is appropriate to construe this urge as a variant of the universal and elemental instinct for self-preservation. It is related to what we commonly think of as "self-preservation," however, only in an unfamiliarly literal sense—that is, in the sense of sustaining not the *life* of the organism but the persistence and vitality of *the self.*

9 Practical reasoning is concerned, at least in part, with the design of effective means for attaining our ends. If it is to have an appropriately settled framework and foundation, it must be grounded in ends that we regard as something more than means to still other ends. There must be certain things that we value and that we pursue for their own sakes. Now it is easy enough to understand how something comes to possess instrumental value. That is just a matter of its being causally efficacious in contributing to the fulfillment of a certain goal. But how is it that things may come to have for us a terminal value that is independent of their usefulness for pursuing further goals? In what acceptable way can our need for final ends be met?

It is love, I believe, that meets this need. It is in coming to love certain things—however this may be caused—that we become bound to final ends by more than an adventitious impulse or a deliberate willful choice.[9] Love is the originating source of terminal value. If we loved nothing, then nothing would possess for us any definitive and inherent worth.

---

[9] In addition to its concern with the design of means, practical reason is also concerned with setting our final ends. It accomplishes this by identifying what it is that we love. This may require significant investigation and analysis. People cannot reliably discover what they love merely by introspection; nor is what they love generally unmistakable in their behavior. Love is a complex configuration of the will, which may be difficult both for the lover and for others to discern.

There would be nothing that we found ourselves in any way constrained to accept as a final end. By its very nature, loving entails both that we regard its objects as valuable in themselves and that we have no choice but to adopt those objects as our final ends. Insofar as love is the creator both of inherent or terminal value and of importance, then, it is the ultimate ground of practical rationality.

There are many philosophers, of course, who claim to the contrary that certain things have an inherent value that is altogether independent of any of our subjective states or conditions. This value does not depend at all, they maintain, upon our feelings or our attitudes, nor does it depend upon our volitional tendencies and dispositions. The position of these philosophers is not truly viable, however, as a response to issues concerning how practical reason may be grounded. Its pertinence to those issues is decisively undermined by its failure to deal with, or even to confront, a fundamental problem.

The fact that a goal has a certain inherent value may be presumed to entail that it is qualified or worthy to be pursued as a final end. This plainly does not entail, however, that anyone has an *obligation* to pursue it as a final end; nor is that entailed even by the stronger assumption that the goal in question has greater inherent value than anything else. It is one thing for a person to assert that a particular object or state of affairs has inherent value, and that there is accordingly some reason for choosing it. But it is another thing entirely for the person to assert of that object or state of affairs that it is or should be important to him, or that he should care about it enough to make it one of his goals. There are many inherently valuable goals in which no one is required to be particularly interested.

The claim that things have independent inherent value does not so much as address, much less answer, the question of how a person's final ends are appropriately to be established. Even if the claim were correct—that is, even if certain things do have a value that is utterly unconditioned by subjective considerations—it would still provide *no account at all* of how people are to select the ends that they will pursue. That question is not immediately about inherent value, but about importance. So far as I can see, it is not possible to deal with it satisfactorily except by referring to what it is— if anything—that people cannot help considering important to themselves. The most fundamental issues of practical reason cannot be resolved, in other words, without an account of what people love.[10]

10 With respect to a rather curious feature, the relationship between the importance to the lover of loving and the importance to him of the interests of his beloved parallels the relationship between final ends and the means by which they may be reached. The fact that something is effective as a means to some final end is ordinarily supposed to entail only that it possesses a certain *instrumental* value; and how valuable that usefulness makes it is presumed to depend upon the value of the end to which it is a means. It is ordinarily also supposed that the value of the final end

---

[10] It might be argued that we are morally obliged to care about certain things, and that these obligations do not depend upon any subjective considerations. But even if it were true that we have such obligations, it would still be necessary to determine how important it is for us to fulfill them. So far as practical reasoning is concerned, the issue of importance is—as suggested in the preceding chapter—more fundamental than the issue of morality.

is in no way dependent upon the value of the means that make its attainment possible. Thus the relationship of derivation between the value of a means and the value of its final end is generally understood to be asymmetric: the value of the means derives from the value of the end, but not vice versa.

This way of construing the relationship may seem to be straightforwardly incontrovertible—a matter of elementary common sense. Nonetheless, it rests upon a mistake. It assumes that the only value that a final end necessarily possesses for us, simply in virtue of the fact that it *is* a final end, must be identical with the value for us of the state of affairs we bring about when we attain that end. In fact, however, this does not exhaust the importance to us of our final ends. They are necessarily valuable in another way as well.

Our goals are not important to us exclusively because we value the states of affairs that they envisage. It is not important to us only to *attain* our final ends. It is also important to us to *have* final ends. This is because without them, there is nothing important for us to do. If we had no goals at which we aimed for their own sakes, there would be no meaningful purpose in any activity in which we might engage. Having final ends is valuable, in other words, as an indispensable condition of our engaging in activity that we regard as truly worthwhile.

Similarly, the value to us of useful activity is never exclusively instrumental. This is because it is *inherently* important for us to engage in activity that is devoted to advancing our goals. For its own sake, as well as for the outcomes at which it aims, we need productive work. Apart from the specific importance of the goals that we happen to pursue, it is important for us to have something that we consider it worthwhile to do.

It turns out, then, that instrumentally valuable activity, precisely because it is useful, necessarily also possesses intrinsic value. And, by the same token, intrinsically valuable final ends necessarily are instrumentally valuable precisely in virtue of being essential conditions for attaining the intrinsically valuable goal of having something worthwhile to do. Despite the air of paradox, we may fairly say that final ends are instrumentally valuable just because they are terminally valuable, and that effective means to the attainment of final ends are intrinsically valuable just because of their instrumental value.

There is a similar structure in the reciprocal relationship between the importance to us of loving and the importance to us of what we love. Just as a means is subordinated to its end, the activity of the lover is subordinated to the interests of his beloved. It is only because of this subordination, moreover, that loving is important to us for its own sake. The inherent importance of loving is due precisely to the fact that loving consists essentially in being devoted to the well-being of what we love. The value of loving to the lover derives from his dedication to his beloved. As for the importance of the beloved, the lover cares about what he loves for its own sake. Its well-being is inherently important to him. In addition, however, what he loves necessarily possesses an instrumental value for him, in virtue of the fact that it is a necessary condition of his enjoying the inherently important activity of loving it.

11 This may make it seem difficult to understand how the attitude of a lover toward his beloved can be entirely disinterested. After all, the beloved provides the lover with an essential condition for achieving an end—loving—that is intrinsically important to him. What he loves makes

it possible for him to acquire the benefit that loving provides, and to avoid the emptiness of a life in which he has nothing to love. Thus the lover seems inevitably to profit from, and hence to make use of, his beloved. Is it not clear, then, that love must inevitably be self-serving? How is it possible to avoid concluding that it can never be altogether selfless or disinterested?

That conclusion would be too hasty. Consider a man who tells a woman that his love for her is what gives meaning and value to his life. Loving her, he says, is for him the only thing that makes living worthwhile. The woman is unlikely to feel (assuming she actually believes this) that what the man is telling her implies that he does not really love her at all, and that he cares about her only because it makes him feel good. From his declaration that his love for her fulfills a deep need of his life, she will surely not conclude that he is making use of her. Indeed, she will naturally take him to be conveying just the opposite. It will be clear to her that what he is saying implies that he values her for herself, and not merely as a means to his own advantage.

It is possible, of course, that the man is a phony. It is also possible that, although he believes he is telling the truth about himself, he doesn't really know what he is talking about. Let us assume, however, that his professions of love and of its importance to him are not only sincere but also correct. In that case, it would be perverse to infer from them that he is using the woman as a means to the satisfaction of his own interests. The fact that loving her is so important to him is entirely consistent with his being unequivocally wholehearted and selfless in his devotion to her interests. The deep importance to him of loving her hardly entails the absurd consequence that he does not really love her at all.

The appearance of conflict between pursuing one's own interests and being selflessly devoted to the interests of another is dispelled once we appreciate that what serves the self-interest of the lover is nothing other than his selflessness. It is only if his love is genuine, needless to say, that it can have the importance for him that loving entails. Therefore, insofar as loving is important to him, maintaining the volitional attitudes that constitute loving must be important to him. Now those attitudes consist essentially in caring selflessly about the well-being of a beloved. There is no loving without that. Accordingly, the benefit of loving accrues to a person only to the extent that he cares about his beloved disinterestedly, and not for the sake of any benefit that he may derive either from the beloved or from loving it. He cannot hope to fulfill his own interest in loving unless he puts aside his personal needs and ambitions and dedicates himself to the interests of another.

Any suspicion that this would require an implausibly high-minded readiness for self-sacrifice can be allayed by the recognition that, in the very nature of the case, a lover *identifies himself* with what he loves. In virtue of this identification, protecting the interests of his beloved is necessarily among the lover's own interests. The interests of his beloved are not actually *other* than his at all. They are his interests too. Far from being austerely detached from the fortunes of what he loves, he is personally affected by them. The fact that he cares about his beloved as he does means that his life is enhanced when its interests prevail and that he is harmed when those interests are defeated. The lover is *invested* in his beloved: he profits by its successes, and its failures cause him to suffer. To the extent that he invests himself in what he loves, and in that way identifies with it, its interests are identical with his own. It is hardly surprising, then, that for the lover selflessness and self-interest coincide.

12 The identification of a lover with any of the things that he loves is bound to be, of course, both inexact and less than totally comprehensive. His interests and those of his beloved can never be entirely the same; and it is improbable that they will even be wholly compatible. However important to him a beloved may be, it is unlikely to be the only thing that is important to him. It is unlikely, indeed, to be the only thing that he loves. Thus there is ordinarily a strong possibility that disruptive conflict may arise between the lover's devotion to the well-being of something that he loves and his concern for his other interests.

Loving is risky. Lovers are characteristically vulnerable to profound distress if they must neglect what is required of them by one love in order to meet the requirements of another, or if what they love does not do well. They must therefore be careful. They must try to avoid being caused to love what it would be undesirable for them to love. For an infinite being, whose omnipotence makes it absolutely secure, even the most indiscriminate loving is safe. God need not be cautious. He runs no risks. There is no need for God, out of prudence or anxiety, to forgo any opportunities for loving. For those of us who are less extravagantly endowed, on the other hand, our readiness to love needs to be more mindful and more restrained.

On some accounts, the creative activity of God is mobilized by an entirely inexhaustible and uninhibited love. This love, which is understood as being totally without limit or condition, moves God to desire a plenum of existence in which everything that can conceivably be an object of love is included. God wants to love as much as it is possible to love. He naturally has no fear of loving unwisely or too well. What God desires to create and to love, accordingly, is just Being—of any and every kind whatsoever, and as much as there can be.

To say that the divine love is infinite and unconditional is to say that it is completely indiscriminate. God loves *every-thing*, regardless of its character or its consequences. Now this is tantamount to saying that the creative activity in which God's love of Being is expressed and fulfilled has no motive beyond an unlimitedly promiscuous urge to love without boundary or measure. Insofar as people think of God's essence as love, then, they must suppose that there is no divine providence or purpose that constrains in any way the sheer maximal realization of possibility. If God is love, the universe has no point except simply to be.

Finite creatures like ourselves, of course, cannot afford to be so heedless in our loving. Omnipotent agents are free of all passivity. Nothing can happen to them. Therefore, they have nothing to fear. We, on the other hand, incur substantial vulnerabilities when we love. Consequently, we need to maintain a defensive selectivity and restraint. It is important that we be careful to whom and to what we give our love.

Our lack of immediate voluntary control over our loving is a particular source of danger to us. The fact that we cannot directly and freely determine what we love and what we do not love, simply by making choices and decisions of our own, means that we are often susceptible to being more or less helplessly driven by the necessities that love entails. These necessities may lead us to invest ourselves unwisely. Love may engage us in volitional commitments from which we are unable to withdraw and through which our interests may be severely harmed.

13 Notwithstanding the risks to which the constraining force of love exposes us, that constraint itself contributes significantly to the value for us of loving. It is in some degree precisely because loving does bind our wills that we value it as we do. This may seem implausible, given that we customarily represent ourselves with so much self-congratulatory pride as being dedicated above all to the value of freedom. How could we claim convincingly to cherish freedom and at the same time welcome a condition that entails submission to necessity? However, the appearance of conflict here is misleading. The key to dissipating that appearance lies in the superficially paradoxical but nonetheless authentic circumstance that the necessities with which love binds the will are themselves liberating.

There is a striking and instructive resemblance in this matter between love and reason. Rationality and the capacity to love are the most powerfully emblematic and most highly prized features of human nature. The former guides us most authoritatively in the use of our minds, while the latter provides us with the most compelling motivation in our personal and social conduct. Both are sources of what is distinctively humane and ennobling in us. They dignify our lives. Now it is especially notable that while each imposes upon us a commanding necessity, neither entails for us any sense of impotence or restriction. On the contrary, each characteristically brings with it an experience of liberation and enhancement. When we discover that we have no choice but to accede to irresistible requirements of logic, or to submit to captivating necessities of love, the feeling with which we do so is by no means one of dispirited passivity or confinement. In both cases—whether we are following reason or following our hearts—we are typically conscious of an invigorating release and expansion of ourselves. But how can it be that we find ourselves to have been strengthened, and to have been made somehow less confined or limited, by being deprived of choice?

The explanation is that an encounter either with volitional or with rational necessity eliminates uncertainty. It thereby relaxes the inhibitions and hesitancies of self-doubt. When reason demonstrates what *must* be the case, that puts an end to any irresolution on our part concerning what we are to believe. In his account of the satisfaction he derived from his early study of geometry, Bertrand Russell alludes to "the restfulness of mathematical certainty."[11] Mathematical certainty, like other modes of certainty that are grounded in logically or conceptually necessary truths, is restful because it relieves us from having to contend with disparate tendencies in ourselves concerning what to believe. The issue is settled. We need no longer struggle to make up our minds. As long as we are uncertain, we hold ourselves back. Discovering how things must necessarily be enables us—indeed, it requires us—to give up the debilitating restraint that we impose upon ourselves when we are unsure what to think. Then there is no longer any obstacle to wholehearted belief. Nothing stands in the way of a steady and untroubled conviction. We are released from the blockage of irresolution and can give ourselves to an unimpeded assent.

Similarly, the necessity with which love binds the will puts an end to indecisiveness concerning what to care about. In being captivated by our beloved, we are liberated from the impediments to choice and action that consist either in hav-

---

[11] "My Mental Development," in *The Philosophy of Bertrand Russell*, ed. P. A. Schilpp (The Library of Living Philosophers, 1946), 7.

ing no final ends or in being drawn inconclusively both in one direction and in another. Indifference and unsettled ambivalence, which may radically impair our capacity to choose and to act, are thereby overcome. The fact that we cannot help loving, and that we therefore cannot help being guided by the interests of what we love, helps to ensure that we neither flounder aimlessly nor hold ourselves back from definitive adherence to a meaningful practical course.[12]

The requirements of logic and the needs of a beloved supersede any contrary preferences to which we are less authoritatively inclined. Once the dictatorial regimes of these necessities have been imposed, it is no longer up to us to decide what to care about or what to think. We have no choice in the matter. Logic and love preempt the guidance of our cognitive and volitional activity. They make it impossible for us to exercise, for the sake of other goals that we happen to find appealing, control over the formation of our beliefs and our will.

It may seem, then, that the way in which the necessities of reason and of love liberate us is by freeing us from ourselves. That *is*, in a sense, what they do. The idea is nothing new. The possibility that a person may be liberated through submitting to constraints that are beyond his immediate voluntary control is among the most ancient and persistent themes of our moral and religious traditions. "In His will," Dante wrote, "is our peace."[13] The restfulness that Russell reports having found in the discovery of what reason re-

---

[12] It does not in itself guarantee decisiveness, since the fact that we love something does not settle how much we love it—i.e., whether we love it more or less than other things whose interests may compete for our attention.

[13] *Paradiso* 3.85.

quired of him evidently corresponds, at least up to a point, to the escape from inner disturbance that others profess having discovered through accepting as their own the inexorable will of God.

14 I have maintained that love need not be grounded in any judgment or perception concerning the value of its object. Appreciating the value of an object is not an essential condition for loving it. It is certainly possible, of course, for judgments and perceptions of that sort to arouse love. However, love may be aroused in other ways as well.

On the other hand, a sensitivity to the risks and costs of loving does often motivate people to try to minimize the likelihood that they will come to love things that they regard as not especially valuable. They are disinclined to be bound by love unless they expect that there will be relatively little harm—to themselves, or to whatever else they care about—in the loving. In addition, they naturally prefer to avoid expending the attention and the effort that loving requires unless they consider it desirable for the beloved to flourish.

Furthermore, what a person loves reveals something significant about him. It reflects upon his taste and his character; or it may be taken to do so. People are often judged and evaluated on the basis of what they care about. Therefore pride and a concern for reputation encourage them to see to it, insofar as they can, that what they love is something that they and others regard as valuable.

What a person loves, or what he does not love, may be counted to his credit. Or it may discredit him: it may be taken to show that he has a bad moral character, or that he is shallow, or has poor judgment, or that he is in some other way deficient. One variety of love to which everyone is susceptible, and that is widely regarded as reflecting badly upon the lover—especially if it grips him very powerfully—is love of oneself. A propensity toward self-love may not be universally condemned as outright immoral. However, it is commonly disdained as rather unattractive and as unworthy of particular respect. Right-thinking people suppose that anyone ought to do better with his love than to turn it upon himself.

That is not how things look, though, when they are examined in the light of the general account of love that I have given. In the next chapter, I shall develop a way of understanding self-love that supports an attitude toward self-love quite different from the one I have just sketched. Far from demonstrating a flaw in character or being a sign of weakness, I shall argue, coming to love oneself is the deepest and most essential—and by no means the most readily attainable—achievement of a serious and successful life.

Three

The Dear Self

1 There are some things that practically no one can help caring about. For the most part, this is all to the good. It would generally be agreed that, with regard to many of the things that are almost universally loved, it is in fact desirable that everyone love them. We are encouragingly reassured by the fact that nearly all of us love living, love our children, love being in rewarding relationships with others, and so on. The more or less unlimited incidence of these predilections is, we believe, a benign feature of human nature. It ensures that practically everyone is powerfully committed to a set of what practically everyone recognizes as legitimate and indispensable goods.

There is, however, at least one important exception to this. It is widely presumed that for a person to love himself is so natural as to be more or less unavoidable; but it is also widely presumed that this is not such a good thing. Many people—especially when they imagine that the propensity to self-love is both ubiquitous and essentially ineradicable—believe that this headlong tendency of most of us to love ourselves is a grievously injurious defect of human nature. In their view, it is largely self-love that makes it impossible for us to devote ourselves sufficiently and in a suitable way—that is, selflessly—to other things that we love or that it would be good for us to love. Loving oneself is, they think, a serious and often crippling impediment to caring appropriately not only about the requirements of morality but also about important nonmoral goods and ideals. The allegation that we are too deeply immersed in self-love is frequently offered, indeed, as identifying an almost insurmountable obstacle to our living as we should.

2 Kant is among those who are especially dismayed and discouraged by the supposedly ubiquitous and relentless grip of self-love. The fact that people love themselves troubles him because he sees it as a formidable barrier to the advance of morality. In his view, it almost inevitably means that, regardless of what people may do, their motives when they act will not be the motives that morality requires.

At the beginning of the Second Section of his *Foundations of the Metaphysics of Morals*,[1] Kant reflects upon the circumstance that, as it seems to him, it is practically impossible for us ever to know with any real assurance that what a person has done possesses genuine moral worth. He is struck by how irredeemably uncertain we must always be concerning whether people can properly be regarded as having actually been virtuous. The difficulty that bothers him does not arise from doubts as to our ability to identify which action, in the pertinent circumstances, the laws of morality prescribe. For Kant, that is the easy part. The serious problem in arriving at judicious moral evaluations of what people do lies, as he sees it, in the impenetrable obscurity of human motivation.

Even when it is clear that what a person has done conforms entirely—so far as his overt behavior goes—to all relevant moral requirements, it may nonetheless remain quite unclear whether the person acted virtuously. Indeed, no matter how fully his conduct itself satisfies the commands of the moral law, it may fail to earn him any moral credit. The fact that he performed exactly the actions that duty demanded

---

[1] All quotations from Kant are from Lewis White Beck's edition and translation of this work in *Immanuel Kant, Critique of Practical Reason and Other Writings in Moral Philosophy* (University of Chicago Press, 1949).

does not of itself warrant a judgment that he was morally worthy in acting as he did. Reaching a judgment of that kind is not warranted simply by what a person has done. It must take decisively into account what was actually moving the person as he did it.

According to Kant, there is no moral worth in performing an action when the performance is motivated by nothing more than what you yourself want to do. If the desires that move you to act are desires by which you are moved simply for reasons of your own, it makes no difference whether they are aimed benevolently at the well-being of others or greedily at some vulgar personal advantage. In either case, the critical point is that you are doing what you are doing just because you happen to be inclined to do it.

People with generous inclinations are certainly preferable to people who are selfish. It is certainly no less true that animals that are naturally gentle and undemanding are nicer to have around than animals that are characteristically hostile. Now Kant insists that these oppositions, in the natural tendencies of people and of animals, have no greater *moral* significance in the one case than in the other. Human beings who are naturally moved to be generous are no more morally worthy, in his view, than are those nonhuman creatures whose nature it is to be endearingly compliant and affectionate.

Kant does seem to have a point here. Why should a person be awarded any moral credit for doing something that he does just because he is naturally disposed to do it—in other words, just because he feels like doing it? To be sure, pursuing personal goals is not necessarily wrong. Still, a person's success in governing his conduct in accordance with his own desires can hardly be counted as a notable *moral* achievement. Kant makes just the more or less plausible claim that people cannot sensibly be regarded as morally admirable for doing as they please.

According to his account of the matter, there is only one way to earn real moral credit: namely, by doing the right thing *because* it is the right thing to do. No action is morally worthy, he believes, unless it is performed with a deliberate intention to meet the requirements of morality. In order to reach an accurate moral evaluation of someone on the basis of what the person does, we must therefore know the person's motives in doing it.

For Kant, and of course not only for Kant, this is the hard part. It is very difficult to be certain about precisely what is actually moving someone, on a certain occasion, to act as he does. The psychology of human beings is complex and elusive; the sources of their actions are obscure. We are frequently mistaken, not only about the motives of others, but about our own as well. Thus it is only very rarely (if ever) that we can legitimately be confident that a person is really acting for the sake of duty—in other words, that he is being moved to act by respect for the rational authority of an impersonal moral imperative, rather than by some private inclination or desire.

3 In fact, Kant is convinced that we can *never* be altogether confident of this. In the first place, he believes that it is "absolutely impossible by experience to discern with complete certainty a single case" in which a person acts *solely* for the sake of duty. Moral considerations are *never* the *only* ones by which a person is moved; other incentives and intentions are *always* at work. Furthermore, we can never completely rule out the possibility that it is these other motivating fac-

tors, rather than the claims of duty, that are most effectively moving the person as he acts.

It does sometimes look as though it *must* be morality that is playing the decisive role. There are occasionally circumstances in which it seems that we cannot discover anything that *could* plausibly account for the fact that a certain action is performed, other than the motivating force of certain moral considerations. Even then, however, we may easily be mistaken about what is really going on. As Kant warns, "we cannot by any means conclude with certainty that a secret impulse of self-love, falsely appearing as the idea of duty, was not actually the true determining cause of the will." People are not only complicated and obscure. They are also deceptive. It is not at all uncommon for us to misread others, nor do we enjoy any reliable immunity to illusion and error concerning ourselves.

Kant is not cynical, but he wants to be realistic. His considered judgment is that a "cool observer . . . [is bound] to be doubtful sometimes whether true virtue can really be found anywhere in the world." In saying this, Kant is not being derisive. His basic attitude toward human character is not one of dismissive contempt. As he tries to understand what people are up to, he is quite willing to give them the benefit of the doubt. But only up to a point. "Out of love of humanity," he says, "I am willing to admit that most of our actions are *in accordance with duty*; but, if we look closer at our thoughts and aspirations, we everywhere come upon *the dear self*, which is always salient, and it is this instead of the stern command of duty (which would often require self-denial) which supports our plans."

It is clear enough what Kant has in mind. He doubts that we can ever divert ourselves entirely from being preoccupied with our personal inclinations, or that we can ever thoroughly insulate ourselves from their domineering motivational thrust. It is not our devotion to morality but our interest in following our own inclinations, he believes, that uniformly enjoys the higher priority and that exerts the more conclusive influence on our conduct. We may tell ourselves—in what we suppose to be all sincerity—that our attitudes and our actions are, at least at times, conscientiously designed to respond compliantly to the commands of duty. Kant suspects, however, that in fact they always respond primarily to the pressures of desire. It is our own desires that we care about most dearly. We are inextricably immersed in them, and it is invariably and most urgently by them that we are driven. Even when we do the right thing, we do it basically to satisfy our own impulses and ambitions, and not out of respect for the moral law.

4 According to Kant, the fact that the incitements of self-love are so ubiquitous in our lives, and so compelling, makes it impossible for us to submit virtuously to the moral law. I do not propose to challenge Kant's conception of what being morally worthy requires; nor, for that matter, do I propose to dispute any other element of his moral doctrine. I shall not argue that he is mistaken in his belief that there is an intractably inimical relationship between the requirements of morality and the demands of personal desire. On the other hand, I regard what he says about the self, and about our attitudes toward our selves, as significantly out of focus.

Kant has a reputation for uncompromising moral austerity. It must be said, however, that in the passages from his work that I have quoted, he does not give the impression of being either harshly indifferent to ordinary human feelings or unsympathetic to familiar aspects of human weakness. Indeed, there is something appealingly poignant and rather sweet in his sorrowful allusions to the inherent frailties of human character and to the anxious maneuvers of self-deception in which we attempt to conceal them.

But while Kant's regret concerning the inescapable tendency of human beings to be dear to themselves may be on the whole warmhearted and considerate, what reason is there to suppose that any such attitude of regret is really appropriate? When all is said and done, what is so embarrassing or so unfortunate about our propensity to love ourselves? Why should we regard it with any sort of righteous sorrow or distaste, or presume that it is somehow a dreadful obstacle to the attainment of our most proper goals? Why should we think of self-love as being at all an impediment to the sort of life at which we ought reasonably to aim?

After all, are we not told by an Author whose moral authority compares quite favorably to Kant's that we should love our neighbors *as we love ourselves*? That injunction does not sound like a warning against self-love. It neither declares nor implies that we should love others *instead* of loving ourselves. Indeed, it does not in any way suggest that self-love is an enemy of virtue, or that it is somehow discreditable to hold the self dear. On the contrary, the divine command to love others as we love ourselves might even be taken to convey a positive recommendation of self-love as an especially helpful paradigm—a model or ideal, by which we ought seriously to guide ourselves in the conduct of our practical lives.

No doubt, it might be objected with a certain plausibility that the real meaning of God's injunction is quite different from this. Perhaps when the Bible admonishes us to love others as we love ourselves, it intends just to encourage us to love others with the same intensity, or with the same relentless dedication, that we are disposed to lavish upon ourselves. On this reading, the point is merely that we should bring to our love of others the same wholehearted and persistent devotion that we characteristically display toward the dear self. It is not self-love as such that is offered as a model, in other words, but only the exceptionally fulsome manner in which we typically love ourselves.

Be this as it may, I want to take another look at the love that—it is presumed—people naturally have for themselves. I want to suggest an alternative to Kant's way of understanding what is to be meant by "the dear self." This will throw a rather different light on the significance of self-love and on its value.

5 As I understand self-love, it is quite unlike the attitude that Kant has in mind when he laments that we hold the self too dear. In speaking of those who love themselves, Kant describes people who are motivated predominantly by an interest in satisfying their own inclinations and desires, and who on any particular occasion will naturally be moved to act by whichever of those inclinations and desires happens to be the strongest. Those people are not being driven by what I think of as self-love. Their attachment to the dear self is less like self-love than it is like self-indulgence, and self-indulgence is something else entirely.

The attitudes of love and of indulgence are not only very different. They are often opposed. Parents who love their children take great care, if they are sensible, to avoid being indulgent. Their love does not motivate them to give their children whatever the children happen most to want. Rather, they show their love by being concerned about what is genuinely important to their children—in other words, by aiming to protect and to advance their children's true interests. They take into account what their children want only insofar as doing so helps them to accomplish that goal. Precisely because they do love their children, they decline to do many things that their children would very much like them to do.

In just the same way, a person shows that he loves himself. That is, he shows it by protecting and advancing what he takes to be his own true interests, even when doing so frustrates desires by which he is powerfully moved but that threaten to divert him from that goal. On Kant's account, what the dear self craves is not that it be truly and intelligently loved. It craves merely that its impulses and desires be gratified. In other words, it craves that it be indulged. It is not by self-indulgence, however, that a person manifests his self-love. Genuine love for ourselves, like genuine love for our children, requires conscientious attention of a different kind.

6 Let us consider more closely, then, the nature of self-love. Like love of any variety, love for a person has four main conceptually necessary features. First, it consists most basically in a disinterested concern for the well-being or flourishing of the person who is loved. It is not driven by any ulterior purpose but seeks the good of the beloved as something that is desired for its own sake. Second, love is unlike other modes of disinterested concern for people— such as charity—in that it is ineluctably personal. The lover cannot coherently consider some other individual to be an

adequate substitute for his beloved, regardless of how similar that individual may be to the one he loves. The person who is loved is loved for himself or for herself as such, and not as an instance of a type. Third, the lover identifies with his beloved: that is, he takes the interests of his beloved as his own. Consequently, he benefits or suffers depending upon whether those interests are or are not adequately served. Finally, loving entails constraints upon the will. It is not simply up to us what we love and what we do not love. Love is not a matter of choice but is determined by conditions that are outside our immediate voluntary control.

Given these as defining features of love, it is apparent that self-love—notwithstanding its questionable reputation—is in a certain way the purest of all modes of love. The reader is perhaps likely to presume that I cannot possibly mean this. How could the claim that self-love is the purest kind of love be, in truth, anything more than a whimsical and irresponsible toying with paradox? In fact, however, the exceptional purity of self-love can easily be demonstrated.

The claim is not, of course, that loving oneself is especially noble or that it reflects especially well upon a person's character. Rather, the claim is that love of oneself is purer than other sorts of love because it is in cases of self-love that the love is most likely to be unequivocal and unalloyed. Instances of self-love conform more closely than instances of other kinds of love, in other words, to the criteria that identify what loving essentially is. Love of self may strike us offhand as a degenerate type of love, which is perhaps not altogether genuine as a type of love at all. In fact, however, there is a particularly snug fit between self-love and the conceptually indispensable conditions by which the nature of love is defined.

7 To begin with, it will surely be conceded without too much argument that when a person loves himself, the identification of the lover with his beloved is distinctively robust and uncurtailed. For someone who loves himself, needless to say, his own interests and those of his beloved are identical. His identification with the interests of his beloved obviously need not contend with the discrepancies, the uncertainties, or the hesitations that inevitably occur in other sorts of love.

It is even more obvious that someone who loves himself is devoted to his beloved as a particular individual rather than as an instance or exemplar of some general type. The self-love of a person cannot coherently be considered transferable to an equivalent substitute. Perhaps it might makes sense that a man who loves a certain woman is drawn also to another woman who strikes him as very similar to her. But suppose someone comes to believe that another person resembles him closely. The similarity will hardly tempt him to love the other person as he loves himself. What leads us to love ourselves is something altogether different from our possession of characteristics that might be possessed equally by others.

In the third place, self-love is not merely outside our immediate voluntary control. We are moved more naturally to love ourselves, and more heedlessly, than we are moved to love other things. Moreover, our inclination toward self-love is less susceptible than are other modes of love to being effectively inhibited or blocked by indirect influence and management. While the inclination may not be completely irresistible, it is exceptionally difficult to overcome or to elude. Unlike our love for most things, self-love is not produced by or largely dependent upon adventitious causes, which can

provide us with opportunities to exercise a certain manipula-
tive leverage. It is deeply entrenched in our nature and, to a
very considerable degree, independent of contingencies.

Finally, the unalloyed purity of self-love is almost never
spoiled by the intrusion of any extrinsic or ulterior purpose.
Only rather rarely do we seek our own well-being primarily
because we expect that it will lead to some other good. In
the love that we devote to ourselves, the flourishing of the
beloved is sought—to a greater degree than in other types of
love—not only for its own sake but for its own sake alone.
Perhaps it would flirt too egregiously with the absurd to suggest that self-love may be *selfless*. It is entirely apposite, however, to characterize it as *disinterested*. Indeed, self-love is
nearly always entirely disinterested, in the clear and literal
sense of being motivated by no interests other than those of
the beloved.

8 To illuminate the character of self-love, we may helpfully
invoke, as a suggestive model, the comparably (though
not equally) pure love that parents ordinarily have for their
small children. There are a number of significant respects in
which parental love is closely parallel to the love of people
for themselves. The close similarity between these two sorts
of love is probably due to the extraordinary degree to which
the lover, in cases of each of the two sorts, identifies naturally
and more or less irresistibly with the beloved.

In self-love, there can be no discrepancy between the interests of the self-lover and those of the person to whom
his self-love is devoted. The characteristic identification of
parent with child is generally rather more limited and less
certain. Nevertheless, it is as a rule distinctively extensive
and compelling. After all, the child originates literally within

the bodies of its parents; and parents normally continue even long after a child's birth to experience it as being still, in some less organic way, a part of them. The intimacy and vividness of this connection tends to diminish as the child separates from its parents and goes its own way. Until then, however, and often afterward as well, the scope and the strength of parental identification are exceptional.

Self-love and the loving concern of parents for the interests of their small children are also similar in that not only does each consist in a devotion to the good of the beloved, as of course does genuine love of every kind, but in both cases the devotion is ordinarily not motivated by any extraneous ambition or intent whatever. Parents generally care about the good of their small children in a way that is exclusively non-instrumental. They value it *only* for its own sake. This is also characteristic of the way in which people are devoted to their own good. In neither case is it usual for the lover to anticipate or to intend that his efforts to protect or to advance the interests of his beloved will be useful in bringing about some further benefit as well.

On the other hand, the love of persons other than one's children or oneself is rarely so thoroughly disinterested. It is nearly always mixed up with, if not actually grounded in, a hope to be loved in return or to acquire certain other goods that are distinct from the well-being of the beloved—for instance, companionship, emotional and material security, sexual gratification, prestige, or the like. It is only when the beloved is the lover's child that love is likely to be as free of such calculated or implicit expectations as it is almost invariably free of them in the case of a person's love of himself. It is true that parents normally do hope that their infant children will love them someday; and they may often hope that in time their children will provide them with additional benefits as well. Ordinarily, however, these hopes are not salient; they generally remain inconspicuous, and indeed quite irrelevant, at least as long as the children are very young. It is distinctive of undemanding parental love and of self-love alike, then, that the lover's disinterested concern for the good of his beloved tends to be not merely uncontaminated but even wholly unaccompanied by an interest in any other good.

Finally, parental love and self-love are similar in the practically inescapable power with which they naturally grip us. It is true that there are some unfortunate small children whose parents do not care at all about their well-being. There are also some wantonly indifferent, or severely depressed, or mindlessly self-indulgent individuals who do not care at all about themselves. Cases of these sorts, however, are rare. Moreover, they are so discordant with our fundamental expectations concerning human nature that we generally regard them as pathological. Normal people, we suppose, cannot help being powerfully moved to love their children; and they cannot help being powerfully inclined to love themselves. Our dispositions to be loving parents and to love ourselves are innate. It may not be true that dispositions of both kinds are totally ineradicable. We do expect them, however, to be exceptionally stable. When it comes to our children and to ourselves, we have little tendency to be fickle.

9 So what is, then, the particular character of self-love? In what way does this variety of love manifest itself, and what does it entail? Insofar as a person does genuinely love himself, just what does the loving come to?

In its central reality as a mode of love, self-love is of course no different from love of any other kind. As with every type of love, the heart of it is that the lover cares about the good of his beloved for its own sake. He is disinterestedly concerned to protect and to pursue the true interests of the person whom he loves. Since in this case the beloved person is himself, the interests to which he is devoted by his self-love are his own.

Now those interests, like the true interests of anyone, are governed and defined by what he loves. It is what a person loves that determines what is important to him. Thus it is axiomatic that a person's self-love is simply, at its core, a disinterested concern for whatever it is that the person loves.[2] The most perspicuous characterization of the essential nature of self-love is simply that someone who loves himself displays and demonstrates that love just by loving what he loves.

The objects of self-love cannot very helpfully be understood, accordingly, as being uniformly of a single type—namely, objects each of which can appropriately be identified or characterized as a "self." There must be something else that a person loves—something that cannot reasonably, or even intelligibly, be identified as his "self"—in order for there to be anything at all to which his self-love is actually devoted. What is commonly referred to as love by people of themselves is never primary; not, at least, if it is construed in a simplistically literal way. This love is necessarily derivative from, or constructed out of, the love that people have for things that are not identical with themselves. Perhaps, then,

---

[2] The situation is actually not quite so simple, as will appear in section 12 below.

it cannot be quite correct after all to regard self-love as a condition in which the lover and the beloved are strictly the same. A person cannot love himself except insofar as he loves other things.

This may suggest that the very notion of self-love is so barren as to be useless. The notion seems to amount to nothing more than a mere redundancy, generated by a rather pointless iteration. Given that a devotion to the interests of what is loved constitutes a foundationally necessary element of loving, and given also that a person's interests are determined by what he loves, it follows that the love of a person for himself essentially consists simply in devotion to a set of objects comprising whatever it is that he loves. But if there is something that a person does in fact love, then he is necessarily, of course, already devoted to it. To say that he loves himself too, since it means only that he is indeed devoted to the things that he loves, does not appear to add anything to the statement that he is devoted to those things. Thus self-love seems to collapse into nothing more than a love of the things one loves. People cannot avoid loving themselves, it appears, as long as they love anything at all. If a person loves anything, he necessarily loves himself.

10 However, this is too quick. There is more to be said, for the situation is rather less straightforward than the account I have so far given makes it seem. Two sets of complexities must be considered, each of which has a substantial bearing upon how my account needs to be supplemented or revised and upon how self-love is finally to be understood.

In the first place, there are complexities that arise in connection with the proposition that self-love is essentially dependent upon a love of things other than what might plausibly be referred to as "the self." It is true that self-love is not focused upon any such object. Nevertheless, room must be made for the possibility that a person may in fact love himself even though he actually does not love anything else.

Second, there are complexities that arise in connection with the proposition that a person is necessarily devoted to whatever he loves. To be sure, this proposition is in a certain sense no more than a tautology. Still, there are sometimes difficulties in determining whether a person who loves a certain object is truly devoted to it. These difficulties arise from the fact that people may be divided within themselves, in a way that makes it impossible to say unequivocally what it is that they love and what they do not love.

11 Whether or not self-love entails that people love things that are not identical with themselves, it clearly does not require that they recognize that they love such things. It is always possible that a person loves someone or something without realizing that he does so; and it is also always possible that a person believes that he loves things that in fact he does not love at all. People may love themselves, then, despite being uncertain (or even despite being entirely ignorant) concerning what they love. Love is a configuration of the will, which is constituted by various more or less stable dispositions and constraints. The effectiveness of these dispositions and constraints neither requires nor ensures that the person whom they dispose and constrain is aware of them. He may be quite unaware of, and he may even with considerable assurance deny, the role that they play in governing his attitudes and his conduct.

The ignorance and errors of a person concerning what he loves are no obstacle to self-love. Consider the fact that parents may fail to understand what is genuinely important to their children. Parents frequently are, indeed, badly mistaken as to what is really in their children's interests. This does not imply that they lack love for their children. We would charge them with lacking love for their children only if we believed that they had no serious desire to know what their children's interests are. If parents conscientiously try to understand what is important to their children, that suffices to manifest their love convincingly. Parents love their children as long as they make a genuine effort, however inept or unsuccessful it may be, to understand their children's true interests.

The same is true of self-love. A person who does not know what he loves, and who therefore does not know what his true interests are, may nevertheless demonstrate that he loves himself by making a determined effort to understand what is fundamentally important to him—to become clear about what he loves and what that love requires. This does not imply any deviation from the principle that love requires a concern on the part of the lover for the true interests of what he loves. Being concerned for the true interests of his beloved surely requires that the lover also be moved by a more elementary desire to identify those interests correctly. In order to obey the commands of love, one must first understand what it is that love commands.

12 A more difficult issue pertaining to complexities of the first sort has to do with whether it really is impossible for a person to love himself unless (whether he knows it or not) he already loves something else. At first glance, it may seem obvious that self-love must surely be precluded by the absence of love for something that is not identical with oneself. If love essentially entails a concern for what the beloved loves, it is difficult to see how a person

who loves nothing could possibly be loved either by another person or by himself. For if a person loves nothing, then it seems that there is no object that would provide a focus for the concern of someone who loved him. There appears to be no way in which love for him can be expressed. Since he has no interests that one might lovingly care to protect or to advance, there is apparently nothing for a lover to do.

Referring again to the model of parental love indicates, however, that this analysis is excessively simplistic. It is not only in attempting to identify and to support their children's true interests that parents convincingly manifest love for their children. They may manifest it also by doing what they can to ensure that their children *have* genuine interests. Loving parents do not wish their children to be condemned to lives in which there are no final ends, or in which there are only final ends so paltry that a life structured by them remains on the whole chaotically fragmented and nearly empty of meaning. Accordingly, their concern for the well-being of their children naturally extends, insofar as this may be necessary, both to helping their children become capable of loving and to assisting them in finding things to love. This suggests that a person who loves nothing can nonetheless show that he loves himself by attempting to overcome whatever personal characteristics may impair his capacity to love and by making suitable efforts to find things that he will in fact come to love.

Suppose that someone is attempting sincerely to improve his capacity for loving and to add to the number of things that he loves. Suppose further that he cannot help doing this, and also that he has no ulterior purpose: he is moved by tendencies and inclinations that are not immediately subject to his will, and loving is important to him just for its own sake. Perhaps he is a person who recognizes that he loves nothing in particular, or nothing much beyond survival and its requirements, but who wishes to repair that condition; or he might be a person who does already love much, but who wishes to love more. In either case, to regard his interest in doing what he can to find love as expressing love for himself is no less appropriate than to regard parents as expressing love for their children when they do what they can to help their children find love.

The most rudimentary form of self-love, then, consists in nothing more than the desire of a person to love. That is, it consists in a person's desire to have goals that he must accept as his own and to which he is devoted for their own sakes rather than merely for their instrumental value. When a person desires to love, what he desires is that he be in a position to act with confident and settled purpose. Without such purpose, action cannot be satisfying; it is inevitably, as Aristotle says, "empty and vain." By providing us with final ends, which we value for their own sakes and to which our commitment is not merely voluntary, love saves us both from being inconclusively arbitrary and from squandering our lives in vacuous activity that is fundamentally pointless because, having no definitive goal, it aims at nothing that we really want. Love makes it possible, in other words, for us to engage wholeheartedly in activity that is meaningful. Insofar as self-love is tantamount just to a desire to love, it is simply a desire to be able to count on having meaning in our lives.[3]

---

[3] To the extent that human beings cannot help having this desire, we are constituted to love loving. In that case, to love is innately important to us and is by nature among our true interests. But perhaps it would be reasonable to maintain that loving is important to us, and is among our true interests, whether we love it (or care about it) or not. In that case,

13 The second set of complexities to which I referred above have to do with the possibility that people may sometimes be divided within themselves in such a way that it is impossible to give categorical and univocal answers to questions concerning what they love and what they do not love. It may happen that a person truly loves something but that, at the same time, it is also true that he does not want to love it. Part of him loves it, as we might say, and part of him does not. There is a part of him that is opposed to his loving it, and that wishes he did not love it at all. In a word, the person is ambivalent.

In order for a conflict of this sort to be resolved, so that the person is freed of his ambivalence, it is not necessary that either of his conflicting impulses disappear. It is not even necessary that either of them increase or diminish in strength. Resolution requires only that the person become finally and unequivocally clear as to which side of the conflict *he* is on. The forces mobilized on the other side may then persist with as much intensity as before; but as soon as he has definitively established just where he himself stands, his will is no longer divided and his ambivalence is therefore gone. He has placed himself wholeheartedly behind one of his conflicting impulses, and not at all behind the other.

When this happens, the tendency that the person has become resolved to oppose—by having made a decision, or in some other way—is in a sense extruded and rendered external to him. It is separated from his will and thereby becomes alien to it. Once that has been accomplished, the conflict

---

some modification would be required in the formulation of my earlier claims concerning the relationships between loving, importance, and interests.

within him is no longer a conflict in which this now alienated tendency is opposed merely by some contrary inclination. It is opposed by *the person*, in his attempt—as an agent who has become volitionally unified—to withstand its assault upon him. If the alienated tendency proves nonetheless to be too powerful, what it overcomes is not, then, just an opposing inclination. It overcomes the person himself. It is he himself that is defeated, and not merely one of the several tendencies operating within him.

In many cases of this kind, however, the person is unable to make up his mind once and for all which side to be on. He cannot bring himself to identify decisively either with one of the opposing tendencies of his will or with the other. He cannot settle conclusively whether to stand behind his tendency to love or behind his desire to undermine that tendency and to refrain from loving. He does not know which of these contending forces he would, in the end, prefer to prevail. With respect to each of the conflicting inclinations that he finds within himself, he is uncertain whether to oppose it or to join himself to it.

In such cases, the person is volitionally fragmented. His will is unstable and incoherent, moving him in contrary directions simultaneously or in a disorderly sequence. He suffers from a radically entrenched ambivalence, in which his will remains obstinately undefined and therefore lacks effective guiding authority. As long as he is unable to resolve the conflict by which he is torn, and thus to unify his will, the person is at odds with himself.

Suppose, for example, that he is ambivalent with respect to loving a certain woman. Part of him loves her, but part of him is opposed to loving her; and he himself is undecided concerning which of his two inconstant tendencies he wants to prevail.[4] Now to love himself would be for him to love whatever it is that he loves. But since he is unresolved whether to support his love of the woman, or to identify himself with and to mobilize his energies behind his opposition to that love, he is unresolved as to whether he does truly love her. Thus his will is indeterminate. There is no final unequivocal truth, no straightforward fact of the matter, concerning whether he really loves her or really does not. It is correspondingly indeterminate, then, whether he loves himself. Like his love for the woman, his self-love is irreducibly equivocal. He is as radically ambivalent concerning himself in this matter as he is concerning her.[5]

14 Self-doubt was the originating matrix of modern philosophy, and it has continued to be the source of a considerable part of its energy. For the last three or four hundred years, the theoretical doubts that philosophers have raised about themselves—that is, concerning their cognitive and moral capacities—have defined and nourished their most salient intellectual ambitions and their most fecund inquiries. Apart from that, the various more personal doubts

---

[4] This situation differs from one in which the person's uncertainty whether he loves a woman is a matter of his being unsure what his dispositions and attitudes toward her actually are. The problem of accurately identifying or characterizing the elements of one's psychic condition is not the same as the problem of resolving a psychic conflict.

[5] Like the parents who manifest love for their child by a concern to facilitate the child's loving, this man may manifest love for himself by a concern to resolve his ambivalence regarding the woman. In that case, one might perhaps say that his self-love consists—so far as this aspect of his life goes—in a desire to make it possible for him to love himself (or, presuming that there are already some things that he does unequivocally love, to expand his self-love).

about themselves that are chronically suffered by people in general have been widely influential in shaping the character of our culture. The vitality and flavor of contemporary life have notoriously been impaired and soured by modes of radical ambivalence even more poignant and more urgent than the skeptical inhibitions that Descartes and his successors imposed upon themselves.

Needless to say, the story of ambivalence is a very old story. It did not begin in the modern era. Human beings have contended with divided wills, and with being alienated from themselves, for a long time. Saint Augustine, who wrestled with ambivalence in his own life, understood it as a kind of sickness. Here is how he characterized it:

> The mind orders itself to make an act of will. . . . , but it does not fully will to do this thing and therefore its orders are not fully given. It gives the order only in so far as it wills, and in so far as it does not will the order is not carried out. . . . It is . . . no strange phenomenon partly to will to do something and partly to will not to do it. It is a disease of the mind. . . . So there are two wills in us, because neither by itself is the whole will, and each possesses what the other lacks.[6]

Saint Augustine thought that ambivalence, together with the discomfort and dissatisfaction with oneself that it entails, might have been inflicted upon us by God on account of the original sin. It may be, he says, that its cause "lies in the secret punishment of man and in the penitence which casts a deep shadow on the sons of Adam." With this in mind, he was inclined to suppose that escape from a divided will into a state of volitional unity might be impossible for us without the supernatural assistance of God.

---

[6] This quotation and the next are from *Confessions* 8.9.

If ambivalence is a disease of the mind, the health of
the mind requires a unified will. That is, the mind is
healthy—at least with respect to its volitional faculty—insofar as it is wholehearted. Being wholehearted means having
a will that is undivided. The wholehearted person is fully
settled as to what he wants, and what he cares about. With
regard to any conflict of dispositions or inclinations within
himself, he has no doubts or reservations as to where he
stands. He lends himself to his caring and loving unequivocally and without reserve. Thus his identification with the
volitional configurations that define his final ends is neither
inhibited nor qualified.[7]

This wholehearted identification means that there is no
ambivalence in his attitude toward himself. There is no part
of him—that is, no part with which he identifies—that re-
sists his loving what he loves. There is no equivocation in
his devotion to his beloved. Since he cares wholeheartedly
about the things that are important to him, he can properly
be said to be wholehearted in caring about himself. Insofar
as he is wholehearted in loving those things, in other words,
he wholeheartedly loves himself. His wholehearted self-love
consists in, or is exactly constituted by, the wholeheartedness
of his unified will.

15 To be wholehearted *is* to love oneself. The two are
the same. Kierkegaard used as the title of one of his
books the emphatic declaration "Purity of heart is to will one

---

[7] It is perhaps worth pointing out that being wholehearted does not
entail having a closed mind. The wholehearted person need not be a fa-
natic. Someone who knows without qualification where he stands may
nonetheless be quite ready to give serious attention to reasons for changing
that stand. There is a difference between being confident and being stubborn or obtuse.

thing." Taken too literally, this is inaccurate. People who will only one thing are not being pure; they are only being single-minded. The degree to which a person's heart is pure is not a function of how many things the person wills. Rather, it depends upon how they are willed. What counts is the quality of the will—that is, its integrity—not the quantity of its objects.

People do not achieve purity of heart by becoming narrowly focused. The pure heart is the heart of someone who is volitionally unified, and who is thus fully intact. Purity lies, as Kierkegaard doubtless intended to convey, in wholeheartedness. To the extent that a person is wholehearted, no part of his will is alien or opposed to him. He is not passively intruded upon or imposed upon by any element of it. His heart is pure in the sense that his will is purely his own.

Self-love consists, then, in the purity of a wholehearted will. But so what? What reason is there for us to be particularly interested in wholeheartedness, or eager for it? On what basis should we especially care about purity? Why should we think of self-love as desirable and important? What is so wonderful about integrity and an undivided will?

One thing in favor of an undivided will is that divided wills are inherently self-defeating. Division of the will is a counterpart in the realm of conduct to self-contradiction in the realm of thought. A self-contradictory belief requires us, simultaneously, both to accept and to deny the same judgment. Thus it guarantees cognitive failure. Analogously, conflict within the will precludes behavioral effectiveness, by moving us to act in contrary directions at the same time. Deficiency in wholeheartedness is a kind of irrationality, then, which infects our practical lives and renders them incoherent.

By the same token, enjoying the inner harmony of an un-divided will is tantamount to possessing a fundamental kind of freedom. Insofar as a person loves himself—in other words, to the extent that he is volitionally wholehearted—he does not resist any movements of his own will. He is not at odds with himself; he does not oppose, or seek to impede, the expression in practical reasoning and in conduct of what-ever love his self-love entails. He is free in loving what he loves, at least in the sense that his loving is not obstructed or interfered with by himself.

Self-love has going for it, then, its role in constituting both the structure of volitional rationality and the mode of freedom that this structure of the will ensures. Loving our-selves is desirable and important for us because it is the same thing, more or less, as being satisfied with ourselves. The self-satisfaction to which it is equivalent is not a matter of being smugly complacent; nor does it consist in feeling that we have accomplished something valuable, or that we have been successful in fulfilling our ambitions. Rather, it is a condition in which we willingly accept and endorse our own volitional identity. We are content with the final goals and with the loving by which our will is most penetratingly defined.[8]

---

[8] According to Spinoza, self-love, or being satisfied with ourselves, "is really the highest thing we can hope for" (*Ethics* 4.52S). This does not mean that self-love or self-satisfaction is enough to make people happy, or that it is sufficient to make life good. After all, being satisfied with oneself is consistent with being disappointed at how things turn out, with a recognition that we have failed in what we tried most earnestly to do, and with the unhappiness that such misfortunes naturally bring. There are other good things, then, for which it may also be reasonable to hope: e.g., greater power, more talent, better luck. The fact that we are satisfied with ourselves does not entail being satisfied with our lives. Nevertheless,

16 It might be argued that because self-love as such has no specific content, it cannot possess any inherent and fundamental value. Wholeheartedness is only a structural characteristic, after all, which has to do with volitional unity or integrity. Attributing it to someone does nothing to identify the actual tendencies and directions of his will or to pick out the particular objects that he loves. Moreover, self-love is in itself neutral with respect both to moral and to nonmoral values. It has no essential evaluational vector. A person loves himself insofar as he wholeheartedly loves anything at all. The value of what he loves is irrelevant to the question of whether he is wholehearted in loving it.

This leaves open the possibility that someone may wholeheartedly love what is evaluationally nondescript, or what is bad, or what is evil. Attempts are sometimes made to demonstrate that an unconflicted and unequivocal love of things like that is not possible. Many philosophers and religious thinkers have hoped, and have purported to demonstrate, that a will must be inescapably in conflict with itself unless it is effectively guided and constrained by the requirements of morality. If their arguments were sound, it would mean that only a good will can be genuinely wholehearted.

In fact, however, their arguments are not convincing. It seems to me, indeed, that the project in support of which they argue is hopelessly unpromising. Being wholehearted is quite compatible not only with being morally somewhat imperfect, but even with being dreadfully and irredeemably wicked. Whatever the value and importance of self-love, it does not guarantee even a minimal rectitude. The life of a

---

perhaps Spinoza is right. Loving oneself may well be the "highest" or the most important thing of all.

person who loves himself is enviable on account of its wholeheartedness, but it may not be at all admirable. The function of love is not to make people good. Its function is just to make their lives meaningful, and thus to help make their lives in that way good for them to live.

17 Wholeheartedness is difficult to come by. It is not easy for us to be satisfied with ourselves. We are too susceptible to uncertainty and ambivalence concerning what we love. Saint Augustine regarded the impediments to self-love not only as innate, but as probably having been imbued in us by God. Therefore, he suspected that it would take a miracle to overcome them. My own observation is that certain people tend by nature to be wholehearted, while others tend not to be; and I suspect that whether someone achieves any substantial degree of wholeheartedness in his life depends rather heavily upon genetic and other modes of luck. Perhaps this is not actually so different from what Saint Augustine had in mind when he supposed that it is a matter of divine fiat. In any event, it is obvious that we can no more induce ourselves to love ourselves than we can induce ourselves to love anything else.

And what if it turns out that, when all is said and done, we cannot love ourselves? Suppose that we are unable to overcome the doubts and the difficulties that stand in the way of our being wholehearted, and that we remain helplessly deprived of self-love? Earlier, in the opening chapter of this work, I said that one essential difference between human beings and other animals is that the latter are not reflective. They do not wonder what they are up to, or what to think of themselves; they do not care about what or who they are. In other words, they do not take themselves seriously. We, on the other hand, *can* take ourselves seriously; and often we do. It is in consequence of this, of course, that we are capable of being dissatisfied with ourselves.

Perhaps it is a good idea for us not to take ourselves *too* seriously. I will make the point, in closing, by relating a conversation that I had a number of years ago with a woman (a secretary, not a professional philosopher) who worked in an office not far from mine. I did not know her very well; we were acquainted only casually. But she was quite good looking, I was unmarried at the time, and one day we got to talking a bit more personally than usual. In the course of the conversation, she said that in her opinion the only two things that really matter in an intimate relationship are honesty and a sense of humor. This struck me as sensible, at least as a first approximation, albeit rather commonplace. Before I had a chance to respond, however, she had a second thought that was far less commonplace. "You know," she said, "I'm not really all that sure about honesty. After all, even if they tell you the truth, they change their minds so fast that you can't count on them anyhow."

So here is my advice. Let us say that you are simply unable, no matter what you do or how hard you try, to be wholehearted. Let us say that you find it impossible to overcome your uncertainty and your ambivalence, and that you cannot keep yourself from vacillating back and forth. If it is finally and definitively clear to you that you will always suffer from inhibitions and self-doubt, and that you will never succeed in being fully satisfied with what you are—if true self-love is, for you, really out of the question—at least be sure to hang on to your sense of humor.

Acknowledgment

In 2000, I gave the Romanell–Phi Beta Kappa Lectures in Philosophy at Princeton University, under the general title "Some Thoughts about Norms, Love, and the Goals of Life." I gave the same lectures as the Shearman Lectures, at University College London, in 2001. This book is a somewhat revised version of those lectures.